BEST EVER
FISH &
SEAFOOD

A COLLECTION OF OVER **100** ESSENTIAL RECIPES

This edition published in 2011
LOVE FOOD is an imprint of Parragon Books Ltd

Parragon
Queen Street House
4 Queen Street
Bath BA1 1HE, UK

Copyright © Parragon Books Ltd 2007

ISBN: 978-1-4454-3781-1

Printed in China

Designed by Terry Jeavons & Company

Notes for the Reader
This book uses imperial, metric, and US cup measurements. Follow the same units of measurement throughout; do not mix imperial and metric. All spoon measurements are level: teaspoons are assumed to be 5 ml, and tablespoons are assumed to be 15 ml. Unless otherwise stated, milk is assumed to be whole, eggs and individual vegetables such as potatoes are medium, and pepper is freshly ground black pepper.

The times given are an approximate guide only. Preparation times differ according to the techniques used by different people and the cooking times may also vary from those given as a result of the type of oven used. Optional ingredients, variations or serving suggestions have not been included in the calculations.

Recipes using raw or very lightly cooked eggs should be avoided by infants, the elderly, pregnant women, convalescents, and anyone with a chronic condition. Pregnant and breastfeeding women are advised to avoid eating peanuts and peanut products. Sufferers from nut allergies should be aware that some of the ready-prepared ingredients used in the recipes in this book may contain nuts. Always check the packaging before use.

Picture Acknowledgements
The publisher would like to thank the following for permission to reproduce copyright material on the front cover: Seared salmon with yogurt and mint©Gusto Images/Getty Images

FISH & SEAFOOD

introduction

Fish has so many virtues that it is hard to know where to start listing them!

As a health food, fish is superb. It is high in first-class protein and low in salt. It contains vitamins, including A and D in oil-rich fish, and some of the B vitamins, as well as a whole range of minerals—iron, calcium, copper, magnesium, manganese, phosphorus, potassium, selenium, sodium, iodine, fluorine, and zinc. White fish is low in fat, and the fat in fresh oil-rich fish such as halibut, swordfish, salmon, scallops, and tuna contains high amounts of the polyunsaturated fats called omega-3 fatty acids. These fats are essential to health because they cannot be produced

by the human body, and research shows that they reduce cholesterol absorption and help to lower blood-cholesterol levels, preventing the arteries from clogging, and averting coronary heart diseases.

Omega-3 fatty acids are also believed to help in the prevention of cancers of the breast, prostate, and colon and reduce the inflammation associated with rheumatoid arthritis. They even improve brain function and decrease the risk of dementia, depression, and poor memory.

Fish is the perfect food for today's lifestyle—it is quick and easy to cook, and is both light and substantial. On top of all this, fish is good to eat! There is such an incredible variety of fish available, and so many interesting ways to cook it, that you might forget you are eating a highly nutritious superfood and simply focus on the delicious dishes that you can make with it. It can be cooked very simply—baked, roasted, broiled, grilled, pan-fried or stir-fried—or

added to risottos, paellas, pasta, soups, stews, elegant tarts or homely potato-topped pies. The list is endless.

Whether you are eating fish for the sake of your health, or because you love the taste and convenience of it, enjoy the fabulous recipes in this book!

soups & appetizers

Historically, a formal banquet always included a substantial fish course before the meat was served. Today, with our ever-changing lifestyles and appetites, we are more likely to choose a light, elegant appetizer. Soup is always a good choice, and Breton Fish Soup is a chic, creamy French recipe, while Mexican Fish & Roasted Tomato Soup will get the tastebuds tingling, and Thai Shrimp & Scallop Soup is stylish, yet incredibly quick to make.

Spanish tapas has become popular in recent years—you need to serve a good selection, so there are delicious recipes for Fresh Salmon in Mojo Sauce, Fish & Caper Croquettes, Tuna with Pimiento-stuffed Olives, Mussels with Herb & Garlic Butter, Lime-drizzled Shrimp, and Calamari. Japanese sushi is another trendy appetizer—if you've never made it before, Teriyaki Tuna Pressed Sushi with Green Bean Strips and Scattered Sushi with Shrimp, Crab & Avocado are easy to assemble.

For those occasions when you're out to impress with classic simplicity, serve Salmon Tartare or Gravlax, two dishes where the fish is slowly 'seasoned' rather than cooked, Potted Crab, Shrimp Cocktail, or Blinis, a Russian specialty of buckwheat pancakes topped with sour cream and smoked salmon. Gorgeous!

breton fish soup

ingredients

SERVES 4

2 tsp butter

1 large leek, thinly sliced

2 shallots, finely chopped

4 fl oz/125 ml/$^{1}/_{2}$ cup
    hard cider

10 fl oz/300 ml/1$^{1}/_{4}$ cups fish
    stock

9 oz/250 g potatoes, diced

1 bay leaf

salt

4 tbsp all-purpose flour

/ fl oz/200 ml/scant 1 cup
    milk

7 fl oz/200 ml/scant 1 cup
    heavy cream

2 oz/55 g sorrel leaves

12 oz/350 g skinless
    monkfish or cod fillets, cut
    into 1-inch/2.5-cm pieces

method

1 Melt the butter in a large pan over medium-low heat. Add the leek and shallots, and cook, stirring frequently, for 5 minutes, or until they start to soften. Add the cider and bring to a boil.

2 Stir in the stock, potatoes, and bay leaf with a large pinch of salt (unless the stock is salty) and return to a boil. Reduce the heat, cover, and cook gently for 10 minutes.

3 Put the flour in a small bowl and very slowly whisk in a few tablespoons of the milk to make a thick paste. Stir in a little more milk to make a smooth liquid. Adjust the heat so that the soup bubbles gently. Stir in the flour mixture and cook, stirring frequently, for 5 minutes. Add the remaining milk and half the cream. Cook for an additional 10 minutes, or until the potatoes are tender.

4 Finely chop the sorrel and combine with the remaining cream. Stir into the soup and add the fish. Cook, stirring occasionally, for an additional 3 minutes, or until the monkfish stiffens or the cod just begins to flake. Taste the soup and adjust the seasoning, if necessary. Ladle into warmed bowls and serve.

fish & sweet potato soup

ingredients

SERVES 4

4 tbsp lemon juice

1 fresh red chile, seeded and
finely sliced

pinch of nutmeg

9 oz/250 g white fish fillets,
skinned, rinsed, and dried

1 tbsp vegetable oil

1 onion, chopped

4 scallions, chopped

2 garlic cloves, chopped

1 lb/450 g sweet potatoes,
diced

32 fl oz/1 liter/4 cups
vegetable stock

1 carrot, sliced

5 1/2 oz/150 g white cabbage,
shredded

2 celery stalks, sliced

salt and pepper

crusty bread, to serve

method

1 Put the lemon juice, chile, and nutmeg in a shallow, nonmetallic dish and mix together. Cut the fish fillets into chunks and add to the dish. Turn in the marinade until well coated. Cover with plastic wrap and let marinate in the refrigerator for 30 minutes.

2 Heat the oil in a large pan over medium heat. Add the onion and scallions and cook, stirring frequently, for 4 minutes. Add the garlic and cook, stirring, for 2 minutes.

3 Add the sweet potatoes, stock, salt, and pepper. Bring to a boil, then reduce the heat, cover, and let simmer for 10 minutes. Add the carrot, cabbage, and celery, season again, and let simmer for 8–10 minutes.

4 Let the soup cool slightly, then transfer to a blender or food processor and process until smooth, working in batches if necessary. Return to the pan. Add the fish and marinade and bring gently to a boil. Reduce the heat and let simmer for 10 minutes. Ladle the soup into bowls and serve with crusty bread.

mexican fish & roasted tomato soup

ingredients

SERVES 4

5 ripe tomatoes

5 garlic cloves, unpeeled

32 fl oz/1 liter/4 cups
    fish stock

1 lb 2 oz/500 g red snapper
    fillets, cut into chunks

2–3 tbsp olive oil

1 onion, chopped

2 fresh chiles, seeded and
    thinly sliced

lime wedges, to serve

method

1 Heat a dry, heavy-bottom skillet over high heat, add the tomatoes and garlic cloves, and cook, turning frequently, for 10–15 minutes until the skins are blackened and charred and the flesh is tender, or cook under a preheated hot broiler. Alternatively, put the tomatoes and garlic cloves in a roasting pan and bake in a preheated oven at 375–400°F/190–200°C for 40 minutes.

2 Let the tomatoes and garlic cool, then remove and discard the skins and coarsely chop the flesh, combining it with any juices from the pan. Set aside.

3 Heat the stock in a pan over medium heat until simmering, add the snapper, and cook just until opaque and slightly firm. Remove from the heat and set aside.

4 Heat the oil in a separate pan, add the onion and cook, stirring frequently, for 5 minutes until softened. Strain in the fish cooking liquid, then add the tomatoes and garlic and stir well. Bring to a boil, then reduce the heat and let simmer for 5 minutes to combine the flavors. Add the chiles.

5 Divide chunks of the poached fish among 4 soup bowls, ladle over the hot soup, and serve with lime wedges for squeezing over.

thai shrimp & scallop soup

ingredients

SERVES 4

32 fl oz/1 liter/4 cups
    fish stock
juice of $1/2$ lime
2 tbsp rice wine or sherry
1 leek, sliced
2 shallots, finely chopped
1 tbsp grated fresh gingerroot
1 fresh red chile, seeded and
    finely chopped
8 oz/225 g raw shrimp,
    shelled and deveined
8 oz/225 g live scallops,
    shucked and cleaned
$1^{1}/_{2}$ tbsp chopped fresh
    flat-leaf parsley, plus extra
    to garnish
salt and pepper

method

1 Put the stock, lime juice, rice wine, leek, shallots, gingerroot, and chile in a large pan. Bring to a boil over high heat, then reduce the heat, cover, and let simmer for 10 minutes.

2 Add the shrimp, scallops, and parsley, season with salt and pepper, and cook for 1–2 minutes.

3 Remove the pan from the heat and ladle the soup into warmed serving bowls. Garnish with chopped parsley and serve.

crab & corn soup

ingredients

SERVES 4

4 oz/115 g fresh or frozen
   crabmeat

20 fl oz/625 ml/2^1/$_2$ cups
   water

15 oz/425 g canned
   cream-style corn, drained

^{1}/$_2$ tsp salt

pinch of pepper

2 tsp cornstarch, dissolved in
   2 tbsp water (optional)

1 egg, beaten

method

1 If using frozen crabmeat, blanch the flesh in boiling water for 30 seconds. Remove with a slotted spoon and set aside.

2 In a large pan, bring the water to a boil with the crab and corn and simmer for 2 minutes. Season with the salt and pepper. Stir in the cornstarch, if using, and continue stirring until the soup has thickened. Rapidly stir in the egg and serve.

salmon tartare

ingredients

SERVES 4

1 lb 2 oz/500 g salmon fillet,
    skinned
2 tbsp sea salt
1 tbsp superfine sugar
2 tbsp chopped fresh dill,
    plus extra sprigs to garnish
1 tbsp chopped fresh tarragon
1 tsp Dijon mustard
juice of 1 lemon
salt and pepper

topping

14 oz/400 g/1^3/$_4$ cups
    cream cheese
1 tbsp snipped fresh chives
pinch of paprika

method

1 Put the salmon in a shallow, nonmetallic dish. Combine the sea salt, sugar, and chopped dill in a small bowl, then rub the mixture into the fish until well coated. Season with pepper. Cover with plastic wrap and let chill in the refrigerator for at least 48 hours, turning the salmon once.

2 Put the tarragon in a bowl with the mustard, lemon juice, salt, and pepper. Remove the salmon from the refrigerator, chop into small pieces, and add to the bowl. Stir until the salmon is well coated.

3 To make the topping, put all the topping ingredients in a separate bowl and mix well together. Put a 4-inch/10-cm steel cooking ring or round cookie cutter on each of 4 small serving plates. Divide the salmon among the 4 steel rings so that each ring is half full. Level the surface of each one, then top with the cream cheese mixture. Smooth the surfaces, then carefully remove the steel rings. Garnish with dill sprigs and serve.

gravlax

ingredients

SERVES 8–12

2 salmon fillets, with skin on, about 1 lb/450 g each

6 tbsp coarsely chopped fresh dill

4 oz/115 g/^{3}/$_8$ cup sea salt

1^3/$_4$ oz/50 g/^{1}/$_4$ cup sugar

1 tbsp white peppercorns, coarsely crushed

12 slices brown bread, buttered, to serve

lemon slices and fresh dill sprigs, to garnish

method

1 Rinse the salmon fillets under cold running water and dry with paper towels. Put 1 fillet, skin-side down, in a nonmetallic dish.

2 Mix the dill, sea salt, sugar, and peppercorns together in a small bowl. Spread this mixture over the fillet in the dish and put the second fillet, skin-side up, on top. Put a plate, the same size as the fish, on top and weigh down with 3–4 food cans.

3 Let chill in the refrigerator for 2 days, turning the fish about every 12 hours and basting with any juices that come out of the fish.

4 Remove the salmon from the brine and thinly slice, without slicing the skin, as you would smoked salmon. Cut the buttered bread into triangles and serve with the salmon. Garnish with lemon slices and dill sprigs.

fresh salmon in mojo sauce

ingredients

SERVES 8

4 fresh salmon fillets,
  weighing about
  1 lb 10 oz/750 g in total
salt and pepper
3 tbsp olive oil
1 fresh flat-leaf parsley sprig,
  to garnish

mojo sauce

2 garlic cloves, peeled
2 tsp paprika
1 tsp ground cumin
5 tbsp extra-virgin olive oil
2 tbsp white wine vinegar
salt

method

1 To prepare the mojo sauce, put the garlic, paprika, and cumin in the bowl of a food processor and, using a pulsing action, blend for 1 minute to mix well together. With the motor still running, add 1 tablespoon of the olive oil, drop by drop, through the feeder tube. When it has been added, scrape down the sides of the bowl with a spatula, then very slowly continue to pour in the oil in a thin, steady stream, until all the oil has been added and the sauce has slightly thickened. Add the vinegar and blend for an additional 1 minute. Season the sauce with salt.

2 To prepare the salmon, remove the skin, cut each fillet in half widthwise, then cut lengthwise into 3/4-inch/2-cm-thick slices, discarding any bones. Season the pieces of fish with salt and pepper.

3 Heat the olive oil in a large, heavy-bottom skillet. When hot, add the pieces of fish and cook for about 10 minutes, depending on its thickness, turning occasionally until cooked and browned on both sides.

4 Transfer the salmon to a warmed serving dish, drizzle over some of the mojo sauce, and serve hot, garnished with parsley, and accompanied by the remaining sauce.

salmon & prawn spring rolls with plum sauce

ingredients

SERVES 4

4¹/₂ oz/125 g salmon fillet, skinned, boned and cut into ¹/₈-inch/3-mm cubes

2¹/₄ oz/60 g bean sprouts

2¹/₄ oz/60 g Chinese cabbage, finely shredded

1 oz/25 g scallion, finely chopped

2¹/₄ oz/60 g red bell pepper, seeded and finely sliced into strips

¹/₄ tsp five-spice powder

2¹/₄ oz/60 g cooked shelled shrimp

4 spring roll wrappers, halved widthwise

vegetable oil spray

¹/₄ tsp sesame seeds

plum sauce

3¹/₂ fl oz/100 ml water

2 fl oz/50 ml orange juice

¹/₂ tsp chopped red chile

1 tsp grated gingerroot

7 oz/200 g red plums, pitted weight

1 tsp chopped scallion

1 tsp chopped fresh cilantro

¹/₄ tsp sesame oil

method

1 To make the sauce, put the water, orange juice, chile, gingerroot, and plums into a pan and bring to a boil. Reduce the heat, cover, and let simmer for 10 minutes. Remove from the heat, blend with a hand-held electric blender, or use a food processor, then stir in the scallion, cilantro, and sesame oil. Let cool.

2 Heat a nonstick wok over high heat, add the salmon, and stir-fry for 1 minute. Remove from the wok with a slotted spoon onto a plate. Using the cooking juices from the salmon, stir-fry the vegetables with the five-spice powder until just tender, drain in a colander, then stir in the cooked salmon and shrimp—the mixture should be quite dry to prevent the rolls from becoming soggy.

3 Divide the salmon and vegetable mixture into 8 portions. Spoon a portion along one short edge of each spring roll wrapper and roll up, tucking in the sides.

4 Lay the spring rolls on a nonstick cookie sheet and spray lightly with vegetable oil, sprinkle with sesame seeds and bake in a preheated oven for 12–15 minutes, or until golden brown. Serve the spring rolls with the cold plum sauce separately.

fish & caper croquettes

ingredients

MAKES 12

12 oz/350 g white fish fillets,
   such as cod, haddock or
   monkfish, skinned and
   boned
10 fl oz/300 ml/1¼ cups milk
salt and pepper
4 tbsp olive oil or
   2 oz/55 g butter
2 oz/55 g/scant ½ cup
   all-purpose flour
4 tbsp capers,
   coarsely chopped
1 tsp paprika
1 garlic clove, crushed
1 tsp lemon juice
3 tbsp chopped fresh
   flat-leaf parsley, plus extra
   sprigs to garnish
1 egg, beaten
2 oz/55 g/1 cup fresh white
   bread crumbs
1 tbsp sesame seeds
corn oil, for deep-frying
lemon wedges, to garnish
mayonnaise, to serve

method

1 Put the fish fillets and milk in a large skillet and season with salt and pepper. Bring to a boil, lower the heat and cook, covered, for 8–10 minutes, or until the fish flakes easily. Remove and flake the fish, reserving the milk.

2 Heat the olive oil or butter in a pan. Stir in the flour to form a paste and cook gently, stirring, for 1 minute. Gradually stir in the reserved milk until smooth. Slowly bring to a boil, stirring, until the mixture thickens.

3 Remove from the heat, add the fish, and beat until smooth. Add the capers, paprika, garlic, lemon juice, and parsley, season again and mix well. Transfer to a dish, let cool, and chill, covered, for 2–3 hours.

4 Pour the beaten egg onto a plate. Combine the bread crumbs and sesame seeds on another plate. Divide the fish mixture into 12 portions and form each portion into a 3-inch/7.5-cm sausage shape. Dip each croquette in the beaten egg, then coat it in the bread crumb mixture. Let chill for 1 hour.

5 Heat the oil in a deep-fryer to 350–375°F/ 180–190°C. Cook the croquettes, in batches, for 3 minutes, or until golden brown and crispy. Drain well on paper towels.

6 Serve piping hot, garnished with lemon wedges and parsley sprigs, and accompanied by a bowl of mayonnaise for dipping.

fish cakes

ingredients

SERVES 4

1 lb/450 g skinned white fish
   fillets, cut into cubes
1 egg white
2 kaffir lime leaves, torn
   coarsely
1 tbsp Thai green curry paste
55 g/2 oz green beans,
   chopped finely
1 fresh red chile, seeded and
   chopped finely
bunch of fresh cilantro,
   chopped
vegetable or peanut oil for
   cooking
1 fresh green chile, seeded
   and sliced, to serve

dipping sauce

4 oz/115 g/generous $1/2$ cup
   superfine sugar
2 fl oz/50 ml/$1/4$ cup white
   wine vinegar
1 small carrot, cut into thin
   sticks
2-inch/5-cm piece cucumber,
   peeled, seeded, and cut
   into thin sticks

method

1 Put the fish into a food processor with the egg white, lime leaves, and curry paste, and process until smooth. Scrape the mixture into a bowl and stir in the green beans, red chile, and cilantro.

2 With dampened hands, shape the mixture into small patties, about 2 inches across. Place them on a large plate in a single layer and let chill for 30 minutes.

3 Meanwhile, make the dipping sauce. Put the sugar in a pan with $1^{1}/2$ tablespoons water and the vinegar and heat gently, stirring until the sugar has dissolved. Add the carrot and cucumber, then remove from the heat and let cool.

4 Heat the oil in a skillet and cook the fish cakes, in batches, until golden brown on both sides. Drain on paper towels and keep warm while you cook the remaining batches. If desired, reheat the dipping sauce. Serve the fish cakes immediately with warm or cold dipping sauce, topped with chile slices.

tuna with pimiento-stuffed olives

ingredients

SERVES 6

2 fresh tuna steaks, weighing
   about 9 oz/250 g in total and
   about 1 inch/2.5 cm thick

5 tbsp olive oil

3 tbsp red wine vinegar

4 sprigs of fresh thyme,
   plus extra to garnish

1 bay leaf

salt and pepper

2 tbsp all-purpose flour

1 onion, finely chopped

2 garlic cloves, finely chopped

3 oz/85 g/$^{1}/_{2}$ cup pimiento-
   stuffed green olives, sliced

method

1 Remove the skin from the tuna steaks, then cut the steaks in half along the grain of the fish. Cut each half into $^{1}/_{2}$-inch/1-cm-thick slices against the grain.

2 Put 3 tablespoons of the olive oil and the vinegar in a large, shallow, nonmetallic dish. Strip the leaves from the sprigs of thyme, add these to the dish with the bay leaf, and season with salt and pepper. Add the prepared strips of tuna, cover the dish, and let marinate in the refrigerator overnight.

3 Put the flour in a plastic bag. Remove the tuna strips from the marinade, reserving the marinade for later, add them to the bag of flour and toss well until lightly coated.

4 Heat the remaining olive oil in a large skillet. Add the onion and garlic and cook gently for 5–10 minutes, or until softened and golden brown. Add the tuna strips and cook for 2–5 minutes, turning several times, until the fish becomes opaque. Add the reserved marinade and olives to the skillet and cook for an additional 1–2 minutes, stirring, until the fish is tender and the sauce has thickened.

5 Serve the tuna and olives piping hot, garnished with thyme sprigs.

teriyaki tuna pressed sushi with green bean strips

ingredients

MAKES 15 PIECES

7 oz/200 g sushi-grade tuna
    or tuna fillet, thinly sliced
2 tbsp teriyaki sauce
1 tbsp oil
10 green beans, trimmed and
    cut in half
oil, for cooking
1 tsp toasted sesame seeds
2 tbsp Japanese mayonnaise
pickled ginger and wasabi
    paste, to serve

sushi rice

4^1/$_2$ oz/125 g/generous
    ^{1}/$_2$ cup sushi rice, washed
    under cold running water
    until the water runs clear,
    then drained
5^1/$_2$ fl oz/160 ml/scant ^{3}/$_4$ cup
    water
^{1}/$_2$ piece of kombu
1 tbsp sushi rice seasoning

method

1 Put the sushi rice in a pan with the water and kombu, cover, and bring rapidly to a boil. Remove the kombu, then re-cover, reduce the heat, and let simmer for 10 minutes. Turn off the heat and let the rice stand, covered, for 15 minutes. Put the hot rice in a large, very shallow bowl, pour the seasoning evenly over the surface, and mix it carefully into the rice with a spatula, using quick cutting strokes. Fan the rice with your hand to cool it.

2 Coat the tuna slices in the teriyaki sauce and cook in the oil in a skillet for 1 minute on each side, then cut them into thick strips. Blanch the green beans in boiling water for a minute, then cool under cold running water and drain.

3 Oil a 7-inch/18-cm loose-bottom square cake pan and line it with a piece of plastic wrap large enough to hang over the edges. Oil the plastic wrap and sprinkle in the sesame seeds. Pack the rice into the pan, spread over the mayonnaise, then arrange the tuna and beans in thick, diagonal strips. Cover with plastic wrap, put another pan on top, and weigh down.

4 Let chill for 15 minutes, then loosen the sides of the pan, and pull out the sushi. Cut into 15 pieces with a wet, sharp knife. Serve with pickled ginger and wasabi paste.

scattered sushi with shrimp, crab & avocado

ingredients

SERVES 4

6 large raw shrimp, shelled
   and deveined, tails left on
1 tbsp oil
1 cooked prepared crab
double quantity freshly
   cooked sushi rice
   (see page 32)
juice and grated rind of 1
   lemon
1 ripe avocado, cut into strips
$^1/_2$ cucumber, peeled and cut
   into slices

method

1 Sauté the shrimp for 2 minutes on each side in the oil. Once they are cooked, let cool. Lift the crabmeat out of the shell.

2 Mix the sushi rice with the lemon juice and grated lemon rind.

3 Divide the rice among 4 wooden or ceramic bowls. Arrange the shrimp, crab, avocado, and cucumber on top of the rice.

seafood tempura

ingredients

SERVES 4

8 large raw shrimp, shelled
and deveined

8 squid rings

5$^1/_2$ oz/150 g package
tempura mix

4 live scallops, shucked
and cleaned

7 oz/200 g firm white fish
fillets, cut into strips

vegetable oil, for deep-frying

few drops sesame oil

shoyu (Japanese soy sauce),
to serve

method

1 Make little cuts on the underside of the shrimp to keep them straight while they cook. Remove and discard any membranes from the squid rings.

2 Combine the tempura mix with the amount of water specified on the package instructions in a large bowl until you have a lumpy batter full of air bubbles. Do not try to make the batter smooth or it will be heavy, and use it straight away or it will settle. Drop all the seafood into the batter.

3 Heat the vegetable oil in a deep-fryer, large, heavy-bottom pan, or wok to 350–375°F/ 180–190°C, or until a cube of bread browns in 30 seconds. Add the sesame oil.

4 Deep-fry 2–3 tempura pieces at a time for 2–3 minutes until a very light golden color (if you deep-fry too many pieces at one time, the oil temperature will drop and the batter will be soggy). Remove with a slotted spoon and drain off as much oil as possible, then drain on paper towels for 30 seconds. Serve very hot with shoyu as a dipping sauce.

mussels with herb & garlic butter

ingredients

SERVES 8

1 lb 12 oz/800 g fresh mussels, in their shells
splash of dry white wine
1 bay leaf
3 oz/85 g butter
12 oz/350 g/generous $1/2$ cup fresh white or brown bread crumbs
4 tbsp chopped fresh flat-leaf parsley, plus extra sprigs to garnish
2 tbsp snipped fresh chives
2 garlic cloves, finely chopped
salt and pepper
lemon wedges, to serve

method

1 Scrub the mussel shells under cold running water and pull off any beards. Discard any with broken shells. Tap the remaining mussels and discard any that refuse to close.

2 Put the mussels in a large pan and add the wine and the bay leaf. Cook, covered, over high heat for 5 minutes, shaking the pan occasionally, or until the mussels are opened. Drain the mussels and discard any that remain closed. Shell the mussels, reserving one half of each shell. Arrange the mussels, in their half shells, in a large, shallow, ovenproof serving dish.

3 Melt the butter and pour into a small bowl. Add the bread crumbs, parsley, chives, garlic, salt, and pepper and mix well together. Let stand until the butter has set slightly. Using your fingers or 2 teaspoons, take a large pinch of the herb and butter mixture and use to fill each mussel shell, pressing it down well.

4 To serve, bake the mussels in a preheated oven, 450ºF/230ºC, for 10 minutes, or until hot. Serve immediately, garnished with parsley sprigs, and accompanied by lemon wedges for squeezing over them.

potted crab

ingredients

SERVES 4–6

1 large cooked crab,
    prepared if possible
salt and pepper
whole nutmeg, for grating
2 pinches of cayenne pepper
juice of 1 lemon, or to taste
8 oz/225g lightly salted butter
buttered toast slices and
    lemon wedges, to serve

method

1 If the crab is not already prepared, pick out all the white and brown meat, taking great care to remove all the meat from the claws.

2 Mix the white and brown meat together in a bowl, but do not mash too smoothly. Season well with salt and pepper and add a good grating of nutmeg, the cayenne pepper, and lemon juice.

3 Melt half the butter in a pan over medium heat and carefully stir in the crabmeat. Turn the mixture out into 4–6 small soufflé dishes or ramekins.

4 Melt the remaining butter in a clean pan over medium heat, then continue heating for a few moments until it stops bubbling. Allow the sediment to settle, then carefully pour the clarified butter over the crab mixture. Cover and let chill in the refrigerator for at least 1 hour before serving with buttered toast and lemon wedges. The seal of clarified butter allows the potted crab to be kept for 1–2 days.

caribbean crab cakes

ingredients

MAKES 16

1 potato, peeled and
    cut into chunks
pinch of salt
4 scallions, chopped
1 garlic clove, chopped
1 tbsp chopped fresh thyme
1 tbsp chopped fresh basil
1 tbsp chopped fresh cilantro
8 oz/225 g white crabmeat,
    drained if canned and
    thawed if frozen
$1/2$ tsp Dijon mustard
$1/2$ fresh green chile, seeded
    and finely chopped
1 egg, lightly beaten
pepper
all-purpose flour, for dusting
sunflower oil, for pan-frying
lime wedges, to garnish
cherry tomatoes, to serve

method

1 Put the potato in a small pan and add water to cover and the salt. Bring to a boil, then reduce the heat, cover, and let simmer for 10–15 minutes, or until softened. Drain well, turn into a large bowl, and mash with a potato masher or fork until smooth.

2 Meanwhile, put the scallions, garlic, thyme, basil, and cilantro in a mortar and pound with a pestle until smooth. Add the herb paste to the mashed potato with the crabmeat, mustard, chile, egg, and pepper. Mix well, cover with plastic wrap, and let chill in the refrigerator for 30 minutes.

3 Sprinkle flour onto a large, flat plate. Shape spoonfuls of the crabmeat mixture into small balls with your hands, then flatten slightly and dust with flour, shaking off any excess. Heat the oil in a skillet over high heat, add the crab cakes, and cook in batches for 2–3 minutes on each side until golden. Remove with a slotted spoon and drain on paper towels. Set aside to cool to room temperature.

4 Arrange the crab cakes on a serving dish and garnish with lime wedges. Serve with a bowl of cherry tomatoes.

shrimp cocktail

ingredients

SERVES 4

$^1/_2$ iceberg lettuce, finely
   shredded
5 fl oz/150 ml/$^2/_3$ cup
   mayonnaise
2 tbsp light cream
2 tbsp tomato ketchup
few drops of Tabasco sauce,
   or to taste
juice of $^1/_2$ lemon, or to taste
salt and pepper
6 oz/175 g cooked shelled
   shrimp
paprika, for sprinkling
4 cooked shrimp, in their
   shells, and 4 lemon slices,
   to garnish
thin buttered brown bread
   slices (optional), to serve

method

1 Divide the lettuce among 4 small serving dishes (traditionally, stemmed glass ones, but any small dishes will be fine).

2 Mix the mayonnaise, cream, and tomato ketchup together in a bowl. Add the Tabasco sauce and lemon juice and season well with salt and pepper.

3 Divide the shelled shrimp equally among the dishes and pour over the dressing. Cover and let chill in the refrigerator for 30 minutes.

4 Sprinkle a little paprika over the cocktails and garnish each dish with a shrimp and a lemon slice. Serve the cocktails with slices of brown bread and butter.

lime-drizzled shrimp

ingredients

SERVES 6

4 limes

12 raw jumbo shrimp,
  in their shells

3 tbsp olive oil

2 garlic cloves, finely chopped

splash of fino sherry

salt and pepper

4 tbsp chopped fresh
  flat-leaf parsley

method

1 Grate the rind and squeeze the juice from 2 of the limes. Cut the remaining 2 limes into wedges and set aside for later.

2 To prepare the shrimp, remove the head and legs, leaving the shells and tails intact. Using a sharp knife, make a shallow slit along the back of each shrimp, then pull out the dark vein and discard. Rinse the shrimp under cold water and dry on paper towels.

3 Heat the olive oil in a large, heavy-bottom skillet, then add the garlic and cook for 30 seconds. Add the shrimp and cook for 5 minutes, stirring from time to time, or until they turn pink and start to curl. Mix in the lime rind, juice, and a splash of sherry to moisten, then stir well together.

4 Transfer the cooked shrimp to a serving dish, season with salt and pepper, and sprinkle with the parsley. Serve piping hot, accompanied by the reserved lime wedges for squeezing over the shrimp.

calamari

ingredients

SERVES 6

1 lb/450 g prepared squid
all-purpose flour, for coating
sunflower oil, for deep-frying
salt
lemon wedges, to garnish
garlic mayonnaise, to serve

method

1 Slice the squid into $^1/_2$-inch/1-cm rings and halve the tentacles if large. Rinse under cold running water and dry well with paper towels. Dust the squid rings with flour so that they are lightly coated.

2 Heat the oil in a deep-fat fryer, large, heavy-bottom pan, or wok to 350–375°F/180–190°C, or until a cube of bread browns in 30 seconds. Deep-fry the squid rings in small batches for 2–3 minutes, or until golden brown and crisp all over, turning several times (if you deep-fry too many squid rings at one time, the oil temperature will drop and they will be soggy). Do not overcook as the squid will become tough and rubbery rather than moist and tender.

3 Remove with a slotted spoon and drain well on paper towels. Keep warm in a low oven while you deep-fry the remaining squid rings.

4 Sprinkle the fried squid rings with salt and serve piping hot, garnished with lemon wedges for squeezing over. Accompany with a bowl of garlic mayonnaise for dipping.

blinis

ingredients

MAKES 8

4 oz/115 g/^{3}/4 cup
   buckwheat flour
4 oz/115 g/^{3}/4 cup
   white bread flour
^{1}/6-oz/7-g sachet
   active dry yeast
1 tsp salt
13 fl oz/400 ml/scant
   1^3/4 cups tepid milk
2 eggs, 1 whole and
   1 separated
vegetable oil, for brushing
sour cream and smoked
   salmon, to serve

method

1 Sift both flours into a large, warmed bowl. Stir in the yeast and salt. Beat in the milk, whole egg, and egg yolk until smooth. Cover the bowl and let stand in a warm place for 1 hour.

2 Place the egg white in a spotlessly clean bowl and whisk until soft peaks form. Fold into the batter. Brush a heavy-bottom skillet with oil and set over medium-high heat. When the skillet is hot, pour enough of the batter onto the surface to make a blini about the size of a saucer.

3 When bubbles rise, turn the blini over with a spatula and cook the other side until light brown. Wrap in a clean dish towel to keep warm while cooking the remainder. Serve the warm blinis with sour cream and smoked salmon.

lunch & supper dishes

Fish is just made for lunch and supper dishes. It is light and easily digestible, so you won't find yourself needing to sleep off your lunch or be unable to sleep after supper. It works brilliantly in all sorts of dishes, from thick, delicious chowders to elegant tarts—for speed, try Smoked Salmon, Red Onion & Goat Cheese Tarts or Smoked Salmon, Feta & Dill Parcels, and if you have a little more time to spare, Smoked Fish & Gruyère Soufflé Tart melts in the mouth and tastes out of this world.

Fish marries well with eggs—try Scrambled Eggs with Smoked Salmon, the perfect brunch dish, a really satisfying Salmon Frittata, or Chinese fast food in the form of Shrimp Fu Yung. It is also a favorite ingredient in Mexican snacks such as Fish Tacos Ensenada-style and Fish Burritos.

Fish Cakes and Smoked Fish Pie are great for family meals, needing only a watercress salad or lightly cooked vegetables to accompany. For lunch or supper parties, Seafood in a Light Broth with Vegetables is a very attractive French dish, Potato, Herb & Smoked Salmon Gratin and Scallops in Saffron Sauce are definitely out of the ordinary, and soufflés never fail to draw a gasp of admiration from your guests. The Crab Soufflé will definitely do that!

scrambled eggs with smoked salmon

ingredients

SERVES 4

8 eggs

3 fl oz/90 ml/$^1/_3$ cup
    light cream

2 tbsp chopped fresh dill,
    plus extra for garnishing

salt and pepper

$3^1/_2$ oz/100 g smoked salmon,
    cut into small pieces

2 tbsp butter

slices rustic bread, toasted

method

1 Break the eggs into a large bowl and whisk together with the cream and dill. Season with salt and pepper. Add the smoked salmon and mix to combine.

2 Melt the butter in a large nonstick skillet and pour in the egg and smoked salmon mixture. Using a wooden spatula, gently scrape the egg away from the sides of the skillet as it starts to set and swirl the skillet slightly to allow the uncooked egg to fill the surface.

3 When the eggs are almost cooked but still creamy, remove from the heat and spoon on to the prepared toast. Serve at once, garnished with sprigs of dill.

salmon frittata

ingredients

SERVES 6

9 oz/250 g skinless, boneless
   salmon
3 fresh thyme sprigs
1 fresh parsley sprig plus
   2 tbsp chopped
   fresh parsley
5 black peppercorns
$^1/_2$ small onion, sliced
$^1/_2$ celery stalk, sliced
$^1/_2$ carrot, chopped
6 oz/175 g asparagus spears,
   chopped
3 oz/85 g baby carrots, halved
$3^1/_2$ tbsp butter
1 large onion, finely sliced
1 garlic clove, finely chopped
4 oz/115 g/1 cup fresh or
   frozen peas
8 eggs, lightly beaten
1 tbsp chopped fresh dill
salt and pepper
lemon wedges, to garnish
sour cream, salad, and crusty
   bread, to serve

method

1 Put the salmon in a pan with 1 thyme sprig, the parsley sprig, peppercorns, onion, celery, and carrot. Cover with cold water and bring slowly to a boil. Remove the pan from the heat and let stand for 5 minutes. Remove the fish with a slotted spoon, flake, and set aside. Discard the vegetables and cooking liquid.

2 Bring a large pan of salted water to a boil and blanch the asparagus for 2 minutes. Drain and refresh under cold running water. Blanch the baby carrots for 4 minutes. Drain and refresh under cold running water. Drain both again, pat dry and set aside.

3 Heat half the butter in a large skillet with an ovenproof handle over low-medium heat, add the onion, and cook, stirring, until softened. Add the garlic and remaining thyme and cook, stirring, for 1 minute. Add the asparagus, carrot, and peas and heat through.

4 Transfer to the eggs in a bowl with the chopped parsley, dill, and salmon. Season and stir briefly. Heat the remaining butter in the pan over low heat and return the mixture to the pan. Cover and cook for 10 minutes.

5 Cook under a preheated medium broiler for an additional 5 minutes until set and golden. Serve hot or cold in wedges, topped with a spoonful of sour cream, with salad and crusty bread. Garnish with lemon wedges.

fluffy shrimp omelet

ingredients

SERVES 2–4

4 oz/115 g cooked shelled
   shrimp, thawed if frozen

4 scallions, chopped

2 oz/55 g zucchini, grated

4 eggs, separated

few dashes of Tabasco sauce,
   to taste

3 tbsp milk

salt and pepper

1 tbsp corn or olive oil

1 oz/25 g sharp Cheddar
   cheese, grated

method

1 Pat the shrimp dry with paper towels, then mix with the scallions and zucchini in a bowl and set aside.

2 Using a fork, beat the egg yolks with the Tabasco, milk, salt, and pepper in a separate bowl.

3 Whisk the egg whites in a large bowl until stiff, then gently stir the egg yolk mixture into the egg whites, taking care not to overmix.

4 Heat the oil in a large, nonstick skillet and when hot pour in the egg mixture. Cook over low heat for 4–6 minutes, or until lightly set. Preheat the broiler.

5 Spoon the shrimp mixture on top of the eggs and sprinkle with the cheese. Cook under the preheated broiler for 2–3 minutes, or until set and the top is golden brown. Cut into wedges and serve at once.

shrimp fu yung

ingredients

SERVES 4–6

1 tbsp vegetable or peanut oil

4 oz/115 g raw shrimp,
  shelled and deveined

4 eggs, lightly beaten

1 tsp salt

pinch of white pepper

2 tbsp finely chopped
  Chinese chives

method

1 In a preheated wok or skillet, heat the vegetable or peanut oil and stir-fry the shrimp until they begin to turn pink.

2 Season the beaten eggs with the salt and pepper and pour over the shrimp. Stir-fry for 1 minute, then add the chives.

3 Cook for an additional 4 minutes, stirring all the time, until the eggs are cooked through but still soft in texture, and serve immediately.

crab soufflé

ingredients

SERVES 4–6

1 oz/25 g/¼ cup dried bread
    crumbs

3 tbsp butter, plus extra
    for greasing

1 small onion, finely chopped

1 garlic clove, crushed

2 tsp mustard powder

1 oz/25 g/scant ½ cup
    all-purpose flour

8 fl oz/225 ml/1 cup milk

1¾ oz/50 g Gruyère cheese,
    grated

3 eggs, separated

8 oz/225 g fresh crabmeat,
    thawed if frozen

2 tbsp snipped fresh chives

pinch of cayenne pepper

salt and pepper

method

1 Generously grease a 48-fl oz/1.5-liter/ 6-cup soufflé dish. Add the bread crumbs and shake around the dish to coat completely, shaking out any excess. Set aside on a cookie sheet.

2 Melt the butter in a large pan over low heat, add the onion, and cook, stirring occasionally, for 8 minutes, until softened but not browned. Add the garlic and cook, stirring, for 1 minute. Then add the mustard powder and flour and continue stirring for another minute. Gradually add the milk, stirring constantly, until smooth. Increase the heat slightly and bring slowly to a boil, stirring constantly. Let simmer gently for 2 minutes. Remove from the heat and stir in the cheese. Let cool slightly.

3 Lightly beat in the egg yolks, then fold in the crabmeat, chives, cayenne, salt, and pepper.

4 Whisk the egg whites in a large, clean, greasefree bowl until they hold stiff peaks. Add a large spoonful of the egg whites to the crab mixture and fold together to slacken. Add the remaining egg whites and fold together carefully but thoroughly. Spoon into the prepared dish.

5 Cook in a preheated oven, 400°F/200°C, for 25 minutes until well risen and golden. Serve at once.

seafood in a light broth with vegetables

ingredients

SERVES 4

small pinch of saffron threads

2 oz/55 g unsalted butter

2 carrots, peeled and cut into julienne strips

2 celery stalks, cut into julienne strips

1 zucchini, cut into julienne strips

1 shallot, very finely chopped

2 garlic cloves, very finely chopped

1 bouquet garni

salt and pepper

7 fl oz/200 ml/generous $^3/_4$ cup dry white wine

7 fl oz/200 ml/generous $^3/_4$ cup water

8 pieces of mixed fresh fish, such as salmon fillets and monkfish medallions, or only 1 type of fish, all skin and bones removed, each piece about $4^1/_2$ oz/125 g

9 fl oz/250 ml/generous 1 cup sour cream

fresh chervil sprigs, to garnish

method

1 Put the saffron threads in a small dry skillet over high heat and toast, stirring constantly, for 1 minute, or until you can smell the aroma. Immediately tip out of the pan and set aside.

2 Melt the butter over medium heat in a large skillet with a tight-fitting lid. Add the carrots, celery, zucchini, shallot, garlic, bouquet garni, salt, and pepper. Sauté for 3 minutes, without letting the vegetables color.

3 Meanwhile, bring the wine and water to a boil in a pan over high heat, then boil for 2 minutes. Pour the boiling liquid over the vegetables, then reduce the heat to low and simmer for 5 minutes. Remove from the heat and discard the bouquet garni.

4 Place the fish over the vegetables in a single layer, then cover and simmer for 5 minutes, or until the fish is cooked through and flakes easily. Transfer the fish and vegetables to a warmed bowl and spoon over a little of the poaching liquid. Cover with foil and set aside.

5 Stir the sour cream and saffron threads into the poaching liquid and bring to a boil, stirring. Boil for 3–5 minutes to reduce. Place a mound of vegetables in the center of 4 soup plates and top with the fish. Spoon over the reduced liquid and garnish with the chervil.

smoked fish chowder

ingredients

SERVES 4

2 tbsp butter

1 onion, finely chopped

1 small celery stalk, finely diced

9 oz/250 g potatoes, diced

2 oz/55 g carrots, diced

10 fl oz/300 ml/1¼ cups
   boiling water

salt and pepper

12 oz/350 g smoked cod
   fillets, skinned and cut
   into bite-size pieces

10 fl oz/300 ml/1¼ cups milk

method

1 Melt the butter in a large pan over low heat, add the onion and celery, and cook, stirring frequently, for 5 minutes, or until softened but not browned.

2 Add the potatoes, carrots, water, salt, and pepper. Bring to a boil, then reduce the heat and let simmer for 10 minutes, or until the vegetables are tender. Add the fish to the chowder and cook for an additional 10 minutes.

3 Pour in the milk and heat gently. Taste and adjust the seasoning, if necessary. Serve hot.

caribbean fish chowder

ingredients

SERVES 4

3 tbsp vegetable oil

1 tsp cumin seeds, crushed

1 tsp dried thyme or oregano

1 onion, diced

1/2 green bell pepper, seeded
and diced

1 sweet potato, diced

2–3 fresh green chiles, seeded
and very finely chopped

1 garlic clove, very finely
chopped

32 fl oz/1 liter/4 cups chicken
stock

salt and pepper

14 oz/400 g red snapper
fillets, skinned and cut
into chunks

1 oz/25 g/1/4 cup frozen peas

1 oz/25 g/1/4 cup frozen corn
kernels

4 fl oz/125 ml/1/2 cup light
cream

3 tbsp chopped fresh cilantro,
to garnish

method

1 Heat the oil with the cumin seeds and thyme in a large pan over medium heat. Add the onion, bell pepper, sweet potato, chiles, and garlic and cook, stirring constantly, for 1 minute.

2 Reduce the heat to medium-low, cover, and cook for 10 minutes, or until beginning to soften.

3 Pour in the stock and season generously with salt and pepper. Bring to a boil, then reduce the heat to low-medium, cover, and let simmer for 20 minutes.

4 Add the snapper, peas, corn kernels, and cream. Cook over low heat, uncovered and without boiling, for 7–10 minutes until the fish is just cooked. Serve at once, garnished with chopped cilantro.

potato, herb & smoked salmon gratin

ingredients

SERVES 6

14 fl oz/425 ml/1³/₄ cups milk

3 whole cloves

2 bay leaves

1³/₄ oz/50 g onion, sliced

3 oz/85 g leek, chopped

3¹/₂ oz/100 g lightly cured
    smoked salmon, finely
    sliced into strips

12 oz/350 g potatoes, cut into
    ¹/₁₆-inch/2-mm slices

2 tbsp finely chopped
    fresh chives

2 tbsp finely chopped
    fresh dill

1 tbsp finely chopped fresh
    tarragon

2 tsp wholegrain mustard

pepper

1¹/₄ oz/35 g watercress

method

1 Pour the milk into a large, heavy-bottom pan, add the cloves, bay leaves, onion, leek, and smoked salmon and heat over a low heat. When the milk is just about to reach simmering point, carefully remove the smoked salmon with a slotted spoon and let cool on a plate.

2 Add the potatoes to the milk and stir with a wooden spoon. Return to a simmer and cook, stirring occasionally to prevent the potatoes from sticking, for 12 minutes, or until the potatoes are just beginning to soften and the milk has thickened slightly from the potato starch. Remove the cloves and bay leaves.

3 Add the herbs, mustard, and pepper and stir well. Pour the mixture into a greased and base-lined 7¹/₂-inch/19-cm shallow cake pan. Cover with a layer of greaseproof paper and then foil and bake in a preheated oven, 400°F/200°C, for 30 minutes.

4 Remove from the oven and place a pan on top. Leave to cool for 20 minutes before turning out onto a cookie sheet. Put under a preheated hot broiler to brown the top.

5 Cut the gratin into 6 wedges and serve with the smoked salmon, tossed with watercress.

broiled tuna
& vegetable kabobs

ingredients

SERVES 4

4 tuna steaks, about 5 oz/
    140 g each
2 red onions
12 cherry tomatoes
1 red bell pepper, seeded and
    diced into 1-inch/2.5-cm
    pieces
1 yellow bell pepper, seeded
    and diced into 1-inch/
    2.5-cm pieces
1 zucchini, sliced
1 tbsp chopped fresh oregano
4 tbsp olive oil
pepper
lime wedges, to garnish
selection of salads and
    cooked couscous, new
    potatoes, or bread,
    to serve

method

1 Cut the tuna into 1-inch/2.5-cm dice. Peel the onions, leaving the root intact, and cut each onion lengthwise into 6 wedges.

2 Divide the fish and vegetables evenly among 8 wooden skewers (presoaked to avoid burning) and arrange on the broiler pan.

3 Mix the oregano and oil together in a small bowl. Season with pepper. Lightly brush the kabobs with the oil and cook under a broiler preheated to high for 10–15 minutes or until evenly cooked, turning occasionally. If you cannot fit all the kabobs on the broiler pan at once, cook them in batches, keeping the cooked kabobs warm while cooking the remainder. Alternatively, these kabobs can be cooked on a barbecue.

4 Garnish with lime wedges and serve with a selection of salads, cooked couscous, new potatoes, or bread.

fresh sardines baked with lemon & oregano

ingredients

SERVES 4

2 lemons, plus extra lemon
   wedges, to garnish
12 large fresh sardines,
   cleaned
4 tbsp olive oil
4 tbsp chopped fresh oregano
salt and pepper

method

1 Slice 1 of the lemons, and grate the rind and squeeze the juice from the second lemon.

2 Cut the heads off the sardines. Put the fish in a shallow, ovenproof dish large enough to hold them in a single layer. Put the lemon slices between the fish. Drizzle the lemon juice and oil over the fish. Sprinkle over the lemon rind and oregano and season with salt and pepper.

3 Bake in a preheated oven, 375°F/190°C, for 20–30 minutes until the fish are tender. Serve garnished with lemon wedges.

shrimp & pineapple curry

ingredients

SERVES 4

16 fl oz/500 ml/2 cups
　　coconut cream
$1/2$ fresh pineapple, peeled
　　and chopped
2 tbsp Thai red curry paste
2 tbsp Thai fish sauce
2 tsp sugar
12 oz/350 g raw jumbo shrimp
2 tbsp chopped fresh cilantro
edible flower, to garnish
steamed jasmine rice, to serve

method

1 Place the coconut cream, pineapple, curry paste, fish sauce, and sugar in a large skillet. Heat gently over medium heat until almost boiling. Shell and devein the shrimp. Add the shrimp and chopped cilantro to the skillet and let simmer gently for 3 minutes, or until the shrimp are cooked.

2 Garnish with a fresh flower and serve with steamed jasmine rice.

garlic & herb shrimp

ingredients

SERVES 2

12 raw jumbo shrimp, in
    their shells
juice of $1/2$ lemon
2 garlic cloves, crushed
3 tbsp chopped fresh parsley
1 tbsp chopped fresh dill
3 tbsp softened butter
salt and pepper
lemon wedges, crusty bread,
    and salad, to serve

method

1 Rinse and peel the shrimp. Devein, using a sharp knife to slice along the back from the head end to the tail, and removing the thin black intestine.

2 Mix the lemon juice with the garlic, herbs, and butter to form a paste. Season well with salt and pepper. Spread the paste over the shrimp and let marinate for 30 minutes.

3 Cook the shrimp under a preheated medium broiler for 5–6 minutes. Alternatively, heat a skillet and fry the shrimp in the paste until cooked. Turn out onto hot plates and pour over the juices. Serve at once with lemon wedges, some crusty bread, and salad.

scallops in saffron sauce

ingredients

SERVES 8

5 fl oz/150 ml/²/₃ cup dry
   white wine
5 fl oz/150 ml/²/₃ cup
   fish stock
large pinch of saffron threads
2 lb/900 g shucked scallops,
   preferably large ones,
   with corals
salt and pepper
3 tbsp olive oil
1 small onion, finely chopped
2 garlic cloves, finely chopped
5 fl oz/150 ml/²/₃ cup heavy
   cream
squeeze of lemon juice
chopped fresh flat-leaf
   parsley, to garnish
crusty bread, to serve

method

1 Put the wine, fish stock, and saffron in a pan and bring to a boil. Lower the heat, cover, and let simmer gently for 15 minutes.

2 Meanwhile, remove and discard from each scallop the tough, white muscle that is found opposite the coral, and separate the coral from the scallop. Slice the scallops and corals vertically into thick slices. Dry well on paper towels, then season with salt and pepper.

3 Heat the olive oil in a large, heavy-bottom skillet. Add the onion and garlic and cook until softened and lightly browned. Add the sliced scallops to the skillet and cook gently for 5 minutes, stirring occasionally, or until they turn just opaque. Overcooking the scallops will make them tough and rubbery.

4 Using a slotted spoon, remove the scallops from the skillet and transfer to a warmed plate. Add the saffron liquid to the skillet, bring to a boil, and boil rapidly until reduced to about half. Lower the heat and gradually stir in the cream, just a little at a time. Let simmer gently until the sauce thickens.

5 Return the scallops to the skillet and let simmer for 1–2 minutes just to heat through. Add a squeeze of lemon juice and season with salt and pepper. Serve the scallops hot, garnished with the parsley, with slices or chunks of crusty bread.

fish cakes

ingredients

SERVES 4

1 lb/450 g mealy potatoes,
    such as Russet Burbank,
    Russet Arcadia, or Butte,
    peeled and cut into chunks
1 lb/450 g mixed fish fillets,
    such as cod and salmon,
    skinned
2 tbsp chopped fresh tarragon
grated rind of 1 lemon
2 tbsp heavy cream
salt and pepper
1 tbsp all-purpose flour
1 egg, beaten
4 oz/115 g/1 cup bread
    crumbs, made from day-
    old white or whole wheat
    bread
4 tbsp vegetable oil
lemon wedges, to garnish
watercress salad, to serve

method

1 Bring a large pan of salted water to a boil, add the potatoes, and cook for 15–20 minutes. Drain well, then mash with a potato masher or fork until smooth.

2 Put the fish in a skillet and just cover with water. Bring to a boil over medium heat, then reduce the heat to low, cover, and let simmer gently for 5 minutes until cooked. Remove with a slotted spoon and drain on a plate. When cool enough to handle, flake the fish coarsely into good-size pieces, removing and discarding any bones.

3 Mix the mashed potatoes with the fish, tarragon, lemon rind, and cream in a bowl. Season well with salt and pepper and shape into 4 round cakes or 8 smaller ones.

4 Put the flour, egg, and bread crumbs in separate bowls. Dust the fish cakes with flour, dip into the beaten egg, then coat thoroughly in the bread crumbs. Put on a cookie sheet, cover, and let chill in the refrigerator for at least 30 minutes.

5 Heat the oil in the skillet over medium heat, add the fish cakes, and cook for 5 minutes on each side, turning them with a spatula. Serve hot, garnished with lemon wedges, with a watercress salad to accompany.

fish tacos ensenada-style

ingredients

SERVES 4

1 lb/450 g firm-fleshed white
    fish, such as red snapper
    or cod
$^1/_4$ tsp dried oregano
$^1/_4$ tsp ground cumin
1 tsp mild chili powder
2–3 garlic cloves, finely
    chopped
salt and pepper
3 tbsp all-purpose flour
vegetable oil, for frying
$^1/_4$ red cabbage, thinly sliced
    or shredded
juice of 2 limes
hot pepper sauce or salsa
    to taste
8 soft corn tortillas
1 tbsp chopped fresh cilantro
$^1/_2$ onion, chopped (optional)
salsa of your choice

method

1 Place the fish on a plate and sprinkle with half the oregano, cumin, chili powder, garlic, and salt and pepper, then dust with the flour.

2 Heat the oil in a skillet until it is smoking, then fry the fish in several batches until it is golden on the outside, and just tender in the middle. Remove from the pan and place on paper towels to drain.

3 Combine the cabbage with the remaining oregano, cumin, chili, and garlic, then stir in the lime juice, and season with salt and hot pepper sauce. Set aside.

4 Heat the tortillas in an ungreased nonstick skillet, sprinkling with a few drops of water as they heat; wrap the tortillas in a clean dish towel as you work to keep them warm. Alternatively, heat through in a stack in the pan, alternating the top and bottom tortillas so that they warm evenly.

5 Place some of the warm fried fish in each tortilla, along with a big spoonful of the cabbage salad. Sprinkle with fresh cilantro and onion, if using. Add salsa to taste and serve at once.

fish burritos

ingredients

SERVES 4–6

about 1 lb/450 g firm-fleshed
    white fish fillets, such as
    red snapper or cod, skinned
salt and pepper
1/4 tsp ground cumin
pinch of dried oregano
4 garlic cloves, finely chopped
4 fl oz/125 ml/1/2 cup fish
    stock
juice of 1/2 lemon or lime
8 flour tortillas
2–3 romaine lettuce leaves,
    shredded
2 ripe tomatoes, diced
salsa of your choice
lemon wedges, to garnish

method

1 Season the fish with salt and pepper, then put in a pan with the cumin, oregano, garlic, and enough stock to cover.

2 Bring to a boil and boil for 1 minute. Remove the pan from the heat and let the fish cool in the cooking liquid for about 30 minutes.

3 Remove the fish with a slotted spoon. Flake the fish into bite-size pieces and put in a nonmetallic bowl. Sprinkle with the lemon juice and set aside.

4 Heat the tortillas in a dry nonstick skillet over medium heat, sprinkling with a few drops of water as they heat; wrap in a clean dish towel as you work to keep them warm. Alternatively, heat through in a stack in the pan, alternating the tortillas from the top to the bottom to warm evenly.

5 Arrange some lettuce in the center of 1 tortilla, spoon on a few fish chunks, then sprinkle with a little tomato. Top with some salsa. Repeat with the other tortillas and serve at once, garnished with lemon wedges.

smoked fish pie

ingredients

SERVES 6

1 lb 8 oz/675 g potatoes,
    unpeeled
2 tbsp olive oil
1 onion, finely chopped
1 leek, thinly sliced
1 carrot, diced
1 celery stalk, diced
4 oz/115 g mushrooms, halved
grated rind 1 lemon
12 oz/350 g skinless,
    boneless smoked cod or
    haddock fillet, cubed
12 oz/350 g skinless,
    boneless white fish, cubed
8 oz/225 g cooked
    shelled shrimp
2 tbsp chopped fresh parsley
1 tbsp chopped fresh dill,
    plus sprigs to garnish
salt and pepper
4 tbsp butter, melted
1 oz/25 g Gruyère
    cheese, grated
cooked vegetables, to serve

sauce

4 tbsp butter
4 tbsp all-purpose flour
1 tsp mustard powder
20 fl oz/625 ml/2^1/$_2$ cups milk
3 oz/85 g Gruyère
    cheese, grated

method

1 For the sauce, melt the butter in a large pan, add the flour and mustard powder, and stir until smooth. Cook over very low heat for 2 minutes. Slowly beat in the milk, while heating, until smooth. Let simmer gently for 2 minutes then stir in the cheese until smooth. Remove from the heat and cover the surface of the sauce with plastic wrap. Set aside.

2 Meanwhile, boil the whole potatoes in plenty of salted water for 15 minutes. Drain well and set aside until cool enough to handle.

3 Heat the oil in a clean pan. Add the onion and cook for 5 minutes until softened. Add the leek, carrot, celery, and mushrooms and cook for an additional 10 minutes, or until the vegetables have softened. Stir in the lemon rind and cook briefly. Add the vegetables with the fish, shrimp, parsley, and dill to the sauce. Season and transfer to a greased 56-fl oz/1.75-liter/7-cup casserole dish.

4 Peel the cooled potatoes and grate them coarsely. Mix with the melted butter. Cover the filling with the grated potato and sprinkle with grated Gruyère cheese. Cover loosely with foil and bake in a preheated oven, 400°F/200°C, for 30 minutes. Remove the foil and bake for an additional 30 minutes, or until the topping is golden and the filling is bubbling. Garnish with dill sprigs and serve with vegetables.

smoked fish & gruyère soufflé tart

ingredients

SERVES 6

pie dough

4¹/₂ oz/125 g/scant 1 cup
    all-purpose flour, plus
    extra for dusting

pinch of salt

¹/₂ tsp English mustard
    powder

4 tbsp cold butter, diced, plus
    extra for greasing

1 egg yolk, mixed with a little
    cold water

filling

10 fl oz/300 ml/1¹/₄ cups milk

1 bay leaf

9 oz/250 g skinless, boneless,
    undyed smoked fish

2 tbsp butter

1 oz/25 g/scant ¹/₄ cup all-
    purpose flour

¹/₂ tsp ground nutmeg

white pepper

4¹/₂ oz/125 g Gruyère cheese,
    grated

2 eggs, separated

method

1 Sift the flour, salt, and mustard into a food processor, add the butter, and process to resemble bread crumbs. Add the egg yolk and pulse to bring the dough together. Roll out the dough on a lightly floured counter and use to line a greased 9-inch/23-cm loose-bottom fluted tart pan. Trim the edge, line the tart shell with parchment paper, and fill with dried beans. Let chill for 30 minutes, then bake in a preheated oven, 375°F/190°C, for 10 minutes. Remove the paper and beans, bake for 5 minutes more, then remove from the oven. Increase the temperature to 400°F/200°C.

2 Bring the milk and bay leaf to a simmer in a skillet, add the fish and cook for 3–5 minutes until just cooked. Remove the fish with a slotted spoon, reserving the milk but discarding the bay leaf. Cool then flake the fish.

3 Melt the butter in a pan, stir in the flour, and cook, stirring, for 2–3 minutes. Slowly add the reserved milk and cook, stirring, until thickened. Stir in nutmeg and pepper, then the cheese. Remove from the heat, stir in the egg yolks and fish, and let cool slightly. Whisk the egg whites in a clean bowl until stiff, then fold quickly into the fish mixture. Pour into the tart shell and bake for 15 minutes until risen and browned. Let rest for 10 minutes, then serve.

smoked cod & shrimp tart

ingredients

SERVES 4–6

14 oz/400 g undyed smoked
    cod fillet, rinsed and dried

10 fl oz/300 ml/1¼ cups milk

5½ oz/150 g cooked shelled
    shrimp

7 oz/200 g/scant 1 cup cream
    cheese

3 eggs, beaten

3 tbsp snipped fresh chives

pepper

pie dough

7 oz/200 g/scant 1½ cups
    all-purpose flour

large pinch of salt

3½ oz/100 g margarine,
    diced, plus extra for
    greasing

1 egg yolk

3 tbsp ice-cold water

method

1 To make the pie dough, sift the flour and salt into a mixing bowl, then rub in the margarine until the mixture resembles coarse bread crumbs. Stir in the egg yolk, followed by the water, then bring the mixture together into a ball. Turn out on to a lightly floured counter and knead until smooth. Wrap in plastic wrap and let chill in the refrigerator for 30 minutes.

2 Meanwhile, put the fish into a shallow pan with the milk. Heat gently until simmering and let simmer for 10 minutes, or until just cooked and opaque. Remove the fish with a slotted spoon, let cool a little, then peel away the skin and discard any bones. Flake the fish into large chunks and set aside. Set aside 4 fl oz/125 ml/½ cup of the cooking liquid.

3 Roll out the dough and use to line a lightly greased 10½-inch/26-cm tart pan. Line the tart shell with parchment paper and dried beans and bake in a preheated oven, 400°F/200°C, for 8 minutes. Remove the paper and beans and bake for 5 minutes more.

4 Arrange the fish and shrimp in the tart shell. Beat the cream cheese, reserved cooking liquid, eggs, chives, and pepper in a bowl, then pour over the seafood. Bake for 30 minutes, or until set and golden brown.

smoked salmon, red onion & goat cheese tarts

ingredients

SERVES 4

9 oz/250 g good quality puff
  pastry
all-purpose flour, for rolling
1 egg, lightly beaten with
  1 tbsp milk
1 small red onion, sliced
3¹/₂ oz/100 g goat cheese,
  crumbled
4 slices smoked salmon
pepper

method

1 Roll the puff pastry out to ¹/₄ inch/5 mm thick on a lightly floured counter and cut into 4 even-size squares. Place on an ungreased cookie sheet and brush each square lightly with the egg mixture. Divide the sliced onion evenly among the tarts and top with goat cheese.

2 Bake in a preheated oven, 400°F/200°C, for 20–25 minutes, or until the pastry has risen and is golden brown. Let cool slightly, then top with the slices of smoked salmon and season with pepper. Serve at once.

smoked salmon, feta & dill filo packages

ingredients

MAKES 6 PACKAGES

5 1/2 oz/150 g feta cheese, crumbled

9 oz/250 g/generous 1 cup ricotta cheese

5 1/2 oz/150 g smoked salmon, diced

2 tbsp chopped fresh dill

2 tbsp snipped fresh chives

pepper

12 sheets filo pastry

3 1/2 oz/100 g butter, melted, plus extra for greasing

4 tbsp dried bread crumbs

6 tsp fennel seeds

method

1 In a large bowl, combine the feta, ricotta, smoked salmon, dill, and chives. Season with pepper.

2 Lay out a sheet of pastry on the counter and brush well with melted butter. Sprinkle over 2 teaspoons of the bread crumbs and cover with a second sheet of pastry. Brush with butter and spread a large tablespoon of the salmon mixture on one end of the pastry. Roll the pastry up, folding in the sides, to enclose the salmon completely and create a neat package. Place on a lightly greased cookie sheet, brush the top of the package with butter and sprinkle over 1 teaspoon of the fennel seeds. Repeat with the remaining ingredients to make 6 packages.

3 Bake the packages in a preheated oven, 350°F/180°C, for 25–30 minutes, or until the pastry is golden brown. Serve warm.

monkfish with lime & chile sauce

ingredients

SERVES 4

4 x 4-oz/115-g
  monkfish fillets
1 oz/25 g/¼ cup rice flour
  or cornstarch
6 tbsp vegetable or peanut oil
4 garlic cloves, crushed
2 large fresh red chiles,
  seeded and sliced
2 tsp jaggery or soft light
  brown sugar
juice of 2 limes
grated rind of 1 lime
boiled rice, to serve

method

1 Toss the fish in the flour, shaking off any excess. Heat the oil in a wok and cook the fish on all sides until browned and cooked through, taking care when turning not to break it up.

2 Lift the fish out of the wok and keep warm. Add the garlic and chiles and stir-fry for 1–2 minutes, until they have softened.

3 Add the sugar, the lime juice and rind, and 2–3 tablespoons of water and bring to a boil. Let simmer gently for 1–2 minutes, then spoon the mixture over the fish. Serve immediately with rice.

roast monkfish with romesco sauce

ingredients

SERVES 4

1 monkfish tail, about
   2 lb/900 g, membrane
   removed
2–3 slices serrano ham
olive oil, for brushing
salt and pepper

romesco sauce

1 red bell pepper, halved
   and seeded
4 garlic cloves, unpeeled
2 tomatoes, halved
4 fl oz/125 ml/$\frac{1}{2}$ cup olive oil
1 slice white bread, diced
4 tbsp blanched almonds
1 fresh red chile, seeded and
   chopped
2 shallots, chopped
1 tsp paprika
2 tbsp red wine vinegar
2 tsp sugar
1 tbsp water

method

1 Place the bell pepper, garlic, and tomatoes in a roasting pan and toss with 1 tablespoon of the oil. Roast in a preheated oven, 425°F/220°C, for 20–25 minutes, then cover with a dish towel, and set aside for 10 minutes. Peel off the skins and place the vegetables in a food processor.

2 Heat 1 tablespoon of the remaining oil in a skillet. Cook the bread cubes and almonds over low heat, stirring frequently, until golden. Remove with a slotted spoon and drain on paper towels. Add the chile, shallots, and paprika to the skillet and cook, stirring, for 5 minutes. Transfer both mixtures to the food processor, add the vinegar, sugar, and water, and process to a paste. With the motor running, add the remaining oil through the feeder tube.

3 Reduce the oven temperature to 400°F/200°C. Rinse the monkfish tail and pat it dry. Wrap the ham around the monkfish, brush lightly with oil, and season. Place the fish on a cookie sheet and roast for 20 minutes until the flesh is opaque and flakes easily.

4 Cut through the ham to remove the central bone and produce 2 thick fillets. Cut each fillet into 2 pieces and arrange on plates with a spoonful of romesco sauce. Serve at once.

spanish swordfish stew

ingredients

SERVES 4

4 tbsp olive oil

3 shallots, chopped

2 garlic cloves, chopped

8 oz/225 g canned chopped
tomatoes

1 tbsp tomato paste

1 lb 7 oz/650 g potatoes, sliced

9 fl oz/250 ml/generous 1 cup
vegetable stock

2 tbsp lemon juice

1 red bell pepper, seeded and
chopped

1 orange bell pepper, seeded
and chopped

20 black olives, pitted
and halved

2 lb 4 oz/1 kg swordfish
steak, skinned and cut
into bite-size pieces

salt and pepper

parsley springs and lemon
slices, to garnish

method

1 Heat the oil in a pan over low heat, add the shallots, and cook, stirring frequently, for 4 minutes, or until softened. Add the garlic, tomatoes, and tomato paste, cover, and let simmer gently for 20 minutes.

2 Meanwhile, put the potatoes in an ovenproof casserole with the stock and lemon juice. Bring to a boil, then reduce the heat and add the bell peppers. Cover and cook for 15 minutes.

3 Add the olives, swordfish, and the tomato mixture to the potatoes. Season with salt and pepper. Stir well, then cover and let simmer for 7–10 minutes, or until the swordfish is cooked to your taste.

4 Remove from the heat and garnish with parsley sprigs and lemon slices.

fish with yucatan flavors

ingredients

SERVES 8

4 tbsp annatto seeds, soaked
   in water overnight

3 garlic cloves, finely chopped

1 tbsp mild chili powder

1 tbsp paprika

1 tsp ground cumin

$1/2$ tsp dried oregano

2 tbsp beer or tequila

juice of 1 lime and I orange or
   3 tbsp pineapple juice

2 tbsp olive oil

2 tbsp chopped fresh cilantro

$1/4$ tsp ground cinnamon

$1/4$ tsp ground cloves

2 lb 4 oz/1 kg swordfish
   steaks

banana leaves, for wrapping
   (optional)

orange wedges, to serve

method

1 Drain the annatto, then crush them to a paste in a mortar with a pestle. Work in the garlic, chili powder, paprika, cumin, oregano, beer or tequila, fruit juice, olive oil, fresh cilantro, cinnamon, and cloves. Smear the paste on to the fish and let marinate in the refrigerator for at least 3 hours or overnight.

2 Wrap the fish steaks in banana leaves, tying with string to make packages. Bring water to a boil in a steamer, then add a batch of packages to the top part of the steamer and cook for about 15 minutes or until the fish is cooked through.

3 Alternatively, cook the fish without wrapping in the banana leaves. To cook on the grill, place in a hinged basket, or on a rack, and cook over the hot coals for 5-6 minutes on each side until cooked through; or cook the fish under a preheated broiler for 5-6 minutes on each side until cooked through.

4 Serve with orange wedges for squeezing over the fish.

italian fish

ingredients

SERVES 4

2 tbsp butter

1³/₄ oz/50 g/scant 1 cup
   fresh whole wheat
   bread crumbs

1 heaped tbsp
   chopped walnuts

grated rind and juice of
   2 lemons

2 fresh rosemary sprigs,
   stalks removed

2 tbsp chopped fresh parsley

4 cod fillets, about
   5¹/₂ oz/150 g each

1 garlic clove, crushed

1 small fresh red chile, diced

3 tbsp walnut oil

method

1 Melt the butter in a large pan over low heat, stirring constantly. Remove the pan from the heat and add the bread crumbs, walnuts, the rind and juice of 1 lemon, half the rosemary, and half the parsley, stirring until mixed.

2 Press the bread crumb mixture over the top of the cod fillets. Place the cod fillets in a shallow foil-lined roasting pan and roast in a preheated oven, 400°F/200°C, for 25–30 minutes.

3 Mix the garlic, the remaining lemon rind and juice, rosemary, and parsley, and the chile together in a bowl. Beat in the oil and mix to combine. Drizzle the dressing over the cod steaks as soon as they are cooked.

4 Transfer the fish to warmed serving plates and serve at once.

baked lemon cod with herb sauce

ingredients

SERVES 4

4 thick cod fillets

olive oil, for brushing

8 thin lemon slices

salt and pepper

herb sauce

4 tbsp olive oil

1 garlic clove, crushed

4 tbsp chopped fresh parsley

2 tbsp chopped fresh mint

juice of ½ lemon

method

1 Rinse each cod fillet and pat dry with paper towels, then brush with oil. Place each fillet on a piece of parchment paper that is large enough to encase the fish in a package. Top each fillet with 2 lemon slices and season with salt and pepper. Fold over the parchment paper to encase the fish and bake in a preheated oven, 400°F/200°C, for 20 minutes, or until just cooked and opaque.

2 Meanwhile, to make the herb sauce, put all the ingredients into a food processor and process until finely chopped. Season with salt and pepper.

3 Carefully unfold each package and place it on a serving plate. Pour a spoonful of herb sauce over each piece of fish before serving.

cod with catalan spinach

ingredients

SERVES 4

2 oz/55 g/^{1}/$_2$ cup raisins

2 oz/55 g/^{1}/$_2$ cup pine nuts

4 tbsp extra-virgin olive oil

3 garlic cloves, crushed

1 lb 2 oz/500 g baby spinach
    leaves, rinsed and
    shaken dry

4 cod fillets, each about
    6 oz/175 g

olive oil

salt and pepper

tomato halves and lemon
    wedges, to serve

method

1 Put the raisins in a small bowl, cover with hot water, and set aside to soak for 15 minutes; drain well.

2 Meanwhile, put the pine nuts in a dry skillet over medium-high heat and dry-fry for 1–2 minutes, shaking frequently, until toasted and golden brown: watch closely because they burn quickly.

3 Heat the oil in a large, lidded skillet over medium-high heat. Add the garlic and cook for 2 minutes, or until golden, but not brown. Remove with a slotted spoon and discard.

4 Add the spinach to the oil with only the rinsing water clinging to its leaves. Cover and cook for 4–5 minutes until wilted. Uncover, stir in the drained raisins and pine nuts and continue cooking until all the liquid evaporates. Season with salt and pepper and keep warm.

5 To cook the cod, brush the fillets lightly with oil and sprinkle with salt and pepper. Place under a preheated hot broiler about 4 inches/ 10 cm from the heat and broil for 8–10 minutes until the flesh is opaque and flakes easily.

6 Divide the spinach among 4 plates and place the cod fillets on top. Serve with the tomato halves and lemon wedges.

hake in white wine

ingredients

SERVES 4

about 2 tbsp all-purpose flour

salt and pepper

4 hake fillets, about
    5 oz/140 g each

4 tbsp extra-virgin olive oil

4 fl oz/125 ml/$^1/_2$ cup dry
    white wine, such
    as a white Rioja

2 large garlic cloves,
    very finely chopped

6 scallions, finely sliced

1 oz/25 g fresh parsley,
    very finely chopped

method

1 Spread the flour out on a large, flat plate and season well with salt and pepper. Dredge the skin side of the hake fillets in the seasoned flour, then shake off any excess. Set aside.

2 Heat a shallow, ovenproof casserole over high heat until you can feel the heat rising. Add the oil and heat until a cube of bread sizzles in 30 seconds. Add the hake fillets, skin-side down, and cook for 3 minutes until the skin is golden brown.

3 Turn the fish over and season with salt and pepper. Pour in the wine and add the garlic, scallions, and parsley. Transfer the casserole to a preheated oven, 450°F/230°C, and bake, uncovered, for 5 minutes, or until the flesh flakes easily. Serve the fish straight from the casserole.

nut-crusted halibut

ingredients

SERVES 4

3 tbsp butter, melted

1 lb 10 oz/750 g halibut fillet

2 oz/55 g/generous $^1/_3$ cup
   pistachios, shelled and
   very finely chopped

method

1 Brush the melted butter over the halibut fillet. Spread the nuts out on a large, flat plate. Roll the fish in the nuts, pressing down gently.

2 Preheat a ridged stovetop grill pan over medium heat. Cook the halibut, turning once, for 10 minutes, or until firm but tender—the exact cooking time will depend on the thickness of the fillet.

3 Remove the fish and any loose pistachio pieces from the heat and transfer to a large, warmed serving platter. Serve at once.

garlic-crusted roast fish

ingredients

SERVES 4

2 lb/900 g mealy potatoes

4 fl oz/125 ml/$\frac{1}{2}$ cup milk

2 oz/55 g butter

salt and pepper

4 haddock fillets, about
    8 oz/225 g each

1 tbsp corn oil

4 garlic cloves, finely chopped

2 tbsp chopped fresh parsley,
    to garnish

method

1 Cut the potatoes into chunks and cook in a pan of lightly salted water for 15 minutes, or until tender. Drain well. Mash in the pan until smooth. Set over low heat and beat in the milk, butter, and salt and pepper.

2 Place the haddock fillets in a roasting pan and brush the fish with the oil. Sprinkle the garlic on top, add salt and pepper, then spread with the mashed potatoes. Roast in a preheated oven, 450°F/230°C, for 8–10 minutes, or until the fish is just tender.

3 Meanwhile, preheat the broiler. Transfer the fish to the broiler and cook for about 2 minutes, or until golden brown. Sprinkle with the chopped parsley and serve at once.

fish parcels
with fresh herbs

ingredients

SERVES 4

vegetable oil spray

4 flounder fillets, skinned

6 tbsp chopped fresh herbs,
    such as dill, parsley, chives,
    thyme, or marjoram

finely grated rind and
    juice of 2 lemons

1 small onion, sliced thinly

1 tbsp capers, rinsed
    (optional)

salt and pepper

method

1 Cut 4 large squares of aluminum foil, each large enough to hold a fish and form a packet, and spray with oil.

2 Place each fish fillet on a foil sheet and sprinkle with the herbs, lemon rind and juice, onion, capers (if using), salt, and pepper. Fold the foil to make a secure packet and place on a cookie sheet.

3 Bake the packets in a preheated oven, 375°F/190°C, for 15 minutes, or until tender. Serve the fish piping hot, in their loosely opened packets.

sole à la meunière

ingredients

SERVES 4

4 tbsp all-purpose flour

1 tsp salt

4 x 14-oz/400-g Dover sole,
 cleaned and skinned

$5^{1}/_{2}$ oz/150 g butter

3 tbsp lemon juice

1 tbsp chopped fresh parsley

$^{1}/_{4}$ of a preserved lemon,
 finely chopped (optional)

fresh parsley sprigs, to garnish

lemon wedges, to serve

method

1 Mix the flour with the salt and place on a large plate. Drop the fish into the flour, one at a time, and shake well to remove any excess. Melt 3 tablespoons of the butter in a small pan and use to brush the fish liberally all over. Place the fish under a broiler preheated to medium and cook for 5 minutes on each side.

2 Meanwhile, melt the remaining butter in a pan. Pour cold water into a bowl that is large enough to take the bottom of the pan and keep near by.

3 Heat the butter until it turns a golden brown and begins to smell nutty. Remove at once from the heat and immerse the bottom of the pan in the cold water, to stop the cooking.

4 Place the fillets on individual plates, drizzle with the lemon juice, and sprinkle with the parsley and preserved lemon, if using. Pour over the browned butter, garnish with parsley sprigs, and serve immediately with lemon wedges for squeezing over.

sole florentine

ingredients

SERVES 4

20 fl oz/625 ml/2^1/$_2$ cups milk

2 strips of lemon rind

2 fresh tarragon sprigs

1 fresh bay leaf

^{1}/$_2$ onion, sliced

3^1/$_2$ tbsp butter, plus extra
    for greasing

1^3/$_4$ oz/50 g/generous ^{1}/$_3$ cup
    all-purpose flour

2 tsp mustard powder

1 oz/25 g/^{1}/$_4$ cup freshly
    grated Parmesan cheese

10 fl oz/300 ml/1^1/$_4$ cups
    heavy cream

pinch of freshly grated nutmeg

salt and pepper

1 lb/450 g spinach leaves

4 Dover sole or sole quarter-cut
    fillets (two from each side
    of the fish), about
    1 lb 10 oz/750 g in total

crisp green salad, to serve

method

1 Put the milk, lemon rind, tarragon, bay leaf, and onion in a pan over medium heat and bring slowly to a boil. Remove from the heat and let infuse for 30 minutes.

2 Melt the butter in a separate pan over medium heat and stir in the flour and mustard powder until smooth. Strain the infused milk, discarding the lemon, herbs, and onion. Gradually beat the milk into the butter and flour until smooth. Bring slowly to a boil, stirring constantly, until thickened. Let simmer gently for 2 minutes. Remove from the heat and stir in the cheese, cream, nutmeg, salt, and pepper. Cover the surface of the sauce with parchment paper or plastic wrap. Set aside.

3 Lightly grease a large baking dish. Bring a large pan of salted water to a boil, add the spinach, and blanch for 30 seconds. Drain and refresh under cold running water. Drain again and pat dry with paper towels. Put the spinach in a layer in the base of the dish.

4 Wash and dry the fish fillets. Season with salt and pepper and roll up. Arrange on top of the spinach and pour over the cheese sauce. Bake in a preheated oven, 400°F/200°C, for 35 minutes until bubbling and golden. Serve at once with a green salad.

porgy en papillote

ingredients

SERVES 4

2 porgy, filleted

4 oz/115 g/²/₃ cup pitted
    black olives

12 cherry tomatoes, halved

4 oz/115 g green beans

handful of fresh basil leaves,
    plus extra to garnish

4 lemon slices

4 tsp olive oil

salt and pepper

boiled new potatoes, to serve

method

1 Wash and dry the fish fillets and set aside. Cut 4 large rectangles of parchment paper, each measuring about 18 x 12 inches/ 46 x 30 cm. Fold in half to make a 9 x 12-inch/ 23 x 30-cm rectangle. Cut this into a large heart shape and open out.

2 Lay a porgy fillet on one half of the paper heart. Top with a quarter of the olives, tomatoes, beans, basil, and 1 lemon slice. Drizzle over 1 teaspoon of the oil and season well with salt and pepper.

3 Fold over the other half of the paper and bring the edges of the paper together to enclose. Repeat to make 4 packages. Put the packages on a cookie sheet and cook in a preheated oven, 400°F/200°C, for 15 minutes, or until the fish is tender.

4 Transfer each package to a serving plate, unopened. Garnish with basil leaves and serve with new potatoes.

skate in black butter sauce

ingredients

SERVES 4

4 skate wings, about
6 oz/175 g each
20 fl oz/625 ml/2^1/$_2$ cups
fish stock
8 fl oz/225 ml/1 cup
dry white wine
salt and pepper
4 tbsp butter
2 tbsp lemon juice
2 tsp capers in brine, rinsed
2 tbsp chopped fresh parsley

method

1 Put the fish in a large, heavy-bottom skillet or ovenproof casserole, pour in the stock and wine, and season with salt and pepper. Bring to a boil, then reduce the heat and let simmer for 10–15 minutes until the fish is tender.

2 Meanwhile, melt the butter in a large, heavy-bottom skillet over very low heat and cook until it turns brown but not black. Stir in the lemon juice, capers, and parsley and heat for an additional 1–2 minutes.

3 Transfer the skate wings to warmed serving plates with a spatula, pour the black butter sauce over, and serve at once.

moroccan fish tagine

ingredients

SERVES 4

2 tbsp olive oil

1 large onion, finely chopped

large pinch of saffron threads

$^1/_2$ tsp ground cinnamon

1 tsp ground coriander

$^1/_2$ tsp ground cumin

$^1/_2$ tsp ground turmeric

7 oz/200 g canned chopped
    tomatoes

10 fl oz/300 ml/1$^1/_4$ cups
    fish stock

4 small red snapper, cleaned,
    boned, and heads and
    tails removed

1$^3/_4$ oz/50 g/$^1/_3$ cup pitted
    green olives

1 tbsp chopped preserved
    lemon

3 tbsp chopped fresh cilantro

salt and pepper

freshly prepared couscous,
    to serve

method

1 Heat the oil in a large pan or ovenproof casserole over low heat, add the onion, and cook, stirring occasionally, for 10 minutes until softened, but not browned. Add the saffron, cinnamon, coriander, cumin, and turmeric and cook, stirring constantly, for an additional 30 seconds.

2 Add the tomatoes and stock and stir well. Bring to a boil, then reduce the heat, cover, and let simmer for 15 minutes. Uncover and let simmer for an additional 20–35 minutes, until thickened.

3 Cut each snapper in half, then add the pieces to the pan, pushing them into the sauce. Let simmer gently for an additional 5–6 minutes until the fish is just cooked.

4 Carefully stir in the olives, preserved lemon, and cilantro. Season with salt and pepper and serve with couscous.

blackened snapper with corn papaya relish

ingredients

SERVES 4

4 x 3-oz/85-g snapper fillets
vegetable oil spray
2 lemons, halved, to serve

relish

2 tbsp finely chopped onion
1 tsp sugar
2 tbsp white wine vinegar
2 tbsp cooked or canned corn
    kernels
1/4 tsp finely chopped
    habanero chile or other
    type of chile
3 1/2 fl oz/100 ml/1/3 cup water
1/4 tsp yellow mustard seeds
pinch of ground turmeric
1 tsp cornstarch, blended
    with a little cold water
1 3/4 oz/50 g papaya, cut into
    1/4-inch/5-mm cubes

seasoning mix

1/4 tsp paprika
1/2 tsp onion powder
1/4 tsp dried thyme
1/4 tsp dried oregano
1/4 tsp cayenne pepper
1/4 tsp pepper
1/2 tsp cornstarch

method

1 To make the relish, place the onion, sugar, vinegar, corn, chile, water, mustard seeds, and turmeric into a small pan over medium heat and bring to a boil. Let simmer for 10 minutes, then add the cornstarch mixture, stirring constantly, and cook until it is the required consistency (it will thicken slightly when cooled). Stir in the papaya and let cool.

2 To make the seasoning mix, put all the ingredients into a bowl and mix thoroughly.

3 Sprinkle the seasoning mix over the snapper fillets on both sides and pat into the flesh, then shake off any excess. Lay the fillets on a board.

4 Heat a nonstick skillet over high heat until smoking. Lightly spray both sides of the fillets with oil, then put into the hot skillet and cook for 2 minutes. Turn the fillets and cook all the way through. (If the fillets are thick, finish the cooking under a preheated broiler as the less intense heat will prevent the seasoning mix from burning.) Remove the fish from the skillet.

5 Add the lemon halves, cut-side down, and cook over high heat for 2–5 minutes, until browned. Serve the fillets, topped with relish, on warmed plates, with the lemon halves.

roast red snapper with fennel

ingredients

SERVES 4

9 oz/250 g/2$^1/_4$ cups dried, white bread crumbs

2 tbsp milk

1 fennel bulb, sliced thinly, fronds reserved for garnish

1 tbsp lemon juice

2 tbsp sambuca

1 tbsp chopped fresh thyme

1 bay leaf, crumbled

3 lb 5 oz/1.5 kg whole red snapper, cleaned, scaled, and boned

salt and pepper

3 tbsp olive oil, plus extra for brushing

1 red onion, chopped

10 fl oz/300 ml/1$^1/_4$ cups dry white wine

method

1 Place the bread crumbs in a bowl, add the milk, and set aside for 5 minutes to soak. Place the fennel in another bowl and add the lemon juice, sambuca, thyme, and bay leaf. Squeeze the bread crumbs and add them to the mixture, stirring well.

2 Rinse the fish inside and out under cold running water and pat dry with paper towels. Season with salt and pepper. Spoon the fennel mixture into the cavity, then bind the fish with trussing thread or kitchen string.

3 Brush a large ovenproof dish with olive oil and sprinkle the onion over the bottom. Lay the fish on top and pour in the wine—it should reach about one third of the way up the fish. Drizzle the red snapper with the olive oil and cook in preheated oven, 375°F/190°C, for 25–30 minutes. Baste the fish occasionally with the cooking juices and if it starts to brown, cover with a piece of foil to protect it.

4 Carefully lift out the fish, remove the string, and place on a warmed serving platter. Garnish with the reserved fennel fronds and serve at once.

grilled sea bass with stewed artichokes

ingredients

SERVES 4

4 lb/1.8 kg baby globe
   artichokes

$2^1/_2$ tbsp fresh lemon juice,
   plus the cut halves of
   the lemon

5 fl oz/150 ml/$^2/_3$ cup olive oil

10 garlic cloves, finely sliced

1 tbsp chopped fresh thyme,
   plus extra to garnish

salt and pepper

6 x 4-oz/115-g sea bass fillets

1 tbsp olive oil, for brushing

crusty bread, to serve

method

1 Peel away the tough outer leaves of each artichoke until the yellow-green heart is revealed. Slice off the pointed top at about halfway between the point and the top of the stem. Cut off the stem and pare off what is left of the dark green leaves around the bottom of the artichoke.

2 Submerge the prepared artichokes in water containing the cut halves of the lemon to prevent discoloration. When all the artichokes have been prepared, turn them choke side down and slice thickly.

3 Heat the olive oil in a large pan. Add the artichoke pieces, garlic, thyme, lemon juice, salt, and pepper, cover, and cook the artichokes over low heat for 20–30 minutes, without coloring, until tender.

4 Meanwhile, preheat a ridged stovetop grill pan or light a barbecue. Brush the sea bass fillets with the 1 tablespoon of olive oil and season well. Cook on the grill pan or over hot coals for 3–4 minutes on each side until just tender.

5 Divide the stewed artichokes among individual plates and top each with a fish fillet. Garnish with chopped thyme and serve with crusty bread.

sweet-&-sour sea bass

ingredients

SERVES 2

2¹/₄ oz/60 g bok choy, shredded

1¹/₂ oz/40 g bean sprouts

1¹/₂ oz/40 g shiitake mushrooms, sliced

1¹/₂ oz/40 g oyster mushrooms, torn

³/₄ oz/20 g scallion, finely sliced

1 tsp finely grated gingerroot

1 tbsp finely sliced lemongrass

2 x 3¹/₄-oz/90-g sea bass fillets, skinned and boned

¹/₄ oz/10 g sesame seeds, toasted

sweet-&-sour sauce

3 fl oz/90 ml/scant ¹/₂ cup unsweetened pineapple juice

1 tbsp sugar

1 tbsp red wine vinegar

2 star anise, crushed

3 fl oz/90 ml tomato juice

1 tbsp cornstarch, blended with a little cold water

method

1 Cut 2 x 15-inch/38-cm squares of parchment paper and 2 x 15-inch/38-cm squares of aluminum foil.

2 To make the sauce, heat the pineapple juice, sugar, red wine vinegar, star anise, and tomato juice. Let simmer for 1–2 minutes, then thicken with the cornstarch and water mixture, whisking continuously. Pass through a fine strainer into a small bowl to cool.

3 In a separate large bowl mix together the bok choy, bean sprouts, mushrooms, and scallions, then add the gingerroot and lemongrass. Toss all the ingredients together.

4 Put a square of greaseproof paper on top of a square of foil and fold into a triangle. Open up and place half the vegetable mix in the center, pour half the sweet and sour sauce over the vegetables, and place the sea bass on top. Sprinkle with a few sesame seeds. Close the triangle over the mixture and, starting at the top, fold the right corner and crumple the edges together to form an airtight triangular bag. Repeat to make another bag.

5 Place on a cookie sheet and cook in a preheated oven, 400°F/200°C, for 10 minutes, until the foil bags puff with steam. To serve, place on individual plates and snip open at the table.

seared salmon with quick hollandaise sauce

ingredients

SERVES 4

1 tbsp dried thyme

1 tbsp dried rosemary

1 tbsp dried oregano

1 tbsp mild paprika

1 tsp garlic powder

2 tsp cumin seeds

1 tbsp sea salt

4 salmon fillets, skin removed

1 tbsp vegetable oil

5½ oz/150 g baby spinach

quick hollandaise sauce

3 egg yolks

7 oz/200 g butter

1 tbsp lemon juice

pepper

method

1 Combine the dried herbs, paprika, garlic powder, cumin seeds, and sea salt in a small grinder and process until smooth. Alternatively, grind by hand using a pestle in a mortar. Rub 1 tablespoon of the mixture into the top of each of the salmon fillets.

2 Heat the oil in a large skillet and cook the salmon, spice-side down, for 2–3 minutes, or until golden brown. Turn over and continue cooking until the salmon is cooked to your liking. Do not overcook or the salmon will be dry.

3 To make the hollandaise sauce, place the egg yolks in a blender or food processor. Melt the butter in a small pan until bubbling. With the motor running, gradually add the hot butter in a steady stream until the sauce is thick and creamy. Add the lemon juice, and a little warm water if the sauce is too thick, then season with pepper. Remove from the blender or food processor and keep warm.

4 Divide the baby spinach equally among 4 plates, place the cooked salmon on top, and spoon over the sauce. Serve at once.

roast salmon with lemon & herbs

ingredients

SERVES 4

6 tbsp extra-virgin olive oil

1 onion, sliced

1 leek, sliced

juice of $1/2$ lemon

2 tbsp chopped fresh parsley

2 tbsp chopped fresh dill

salt and pepper

1 lb 2 oz/500 g salmon fillets

freshly cooked baby spinach
   leaves, to serve

lemon slices, to garnish

method

1 Heat 1 tablespoon of the oil in a skillet over medium heat. Add the onion and leek and cook, stirring occasionally, for 4 minutes, or until slightly softened.

2 Meanwhile, place the remaining oil in a small bowl with the lemon juice and herbs and season with salt and pepper. Stir together well. Rinse the fish under cold running water, then pat dry with paper towels. Arrange the fish in a shallow ovenproof dish.

3 Remove the skillet from the heat and spread the onion and leek over the fish. Pour the oil mixture over the top, making sure that everything is well coated. Roast in the center of a preheated oven, 400°F/200°C, for 10 minutes, or until the fish is cooked through.

4 Arrange the cooked spinach on serving plates. Remove the fish and vegetables and serve next to the spinach with the vegetables arranged on top of the fish. Garnish with lemon slices and serve at once.

ginger-marinated salmon & scallops

ingredients

SERVES 4

7 oz/200 g/1 cup brown
    basmati rice

$1/2$ cucumber, diced

4 scallions, sliced

$1/2$ bunch fresh cilantro,
    chopped

1 red bell pepper, seeded
    and diced

1 fresh green chile, seeded
    and thinly sliced

juice of 1 lime

2 tbsp toasted sesame oil

1 lb 2 oz/500 g salmon fillet,
    skinned and cut into chunks

8 scallops, without corals,
    cleaned

$1^3/4$ oz/50 g fresh gingerroot

juice of 1 lemon

1 tbsp olive oil

green salad, to serve

method

1 Bring a large pan of water to a boil, add the rice, and cook for 25 minutes, or until tender. Drain and let cool. Mix the cooled rice with the cucumber, scallions, cilantro, red bell pepper, chile, lime juice, and sesame oil in a bowl. Cover and set aside for the flavors to develop.

2 Meanwhile, put the salmon chunks into a shallow, nonmetallic bowl. Cut each scallop in half and add to the bowl. Using a garlic press or the back of a knife, crush the gingerroot to extract the juice. Mix the ginger juice with the lemon juice and olive oil in a small bowl or pitcher and pour over the seafood. Turn the seafood to coat in the marinade. Cover and let marinate in the refrigerator for 30 minutes. Soak 8 wooden skewers in cold water for 30 minutes, then drain.

3 Thread an equal quantity of the salmon and scallops onto the skewers. Cook under a broiler preheated to high for 3–4 minutes on each side, or until cooked through. Serve the hot seafood skewers with the rice salad and a green salad.

mexican-style salmon

ingredients

SERVES 4

4 salmon steaks, about
6–8 oz/175–225 g each
tomato wedges, 3 finely
chopped scallions, and
shredded lettuce, to serve
lime slices, to garnish

marinade

4 garlic cloves, finely chopped
2 tbsp extra-virgin olive oil
pinch of ground allspice
pinch of ground cinnamon
juice of 2 limes
1–2 tsp marinade from
canned chipotle chiles or
bottled chipotle chile salsa
1/4 tsp ground cumin
pinch of sugar
salt and pepper

method

1 To make the marinade, finely chop the garlic and place in a bowl with the olive oil, allspice, cinnamon, lime juice, chipotle marinade, cumin, and sugar. Add salt and pepper and stir to combine.

2 Coat the salmon with the garlic mixture, then place in a nonmetallic dish. Leave to marinate for at least 1 hour or overnight in the refrigerator.

3 Transfer to a broiler pan and cook under a preheated broiler for 3–4 minutes on each side. Alternatively, cook the salmon over hot coals on a grill until cooked through.

4 To serve, mix the tomato wedges with the scallions. Place the salmon on individual plates and arrange the tomato salad and shredded lettuce alongside. Garnish with lime slices and serve.

roast tuna
with orange & anchovies

ingredients

SERVES 4–6

scant 1 cup freshly squeezed
   orange juice
3 tbsp extra-virgin olive oil
2 oz/55 g anchovy fillets in oil,
   coarsely chopped, with the
   oil reserved
small pinch of dried red
   pepper flakes, or to taste
1 tuna fillet, about
   1 lb 5 oz/600 g
pepper

method

1 Combine the orange juice, 2 tablespoons of
the olive oil, the anchovies and their oil, and
red pepper flakes in a nonmetallic bowl large
enough to hold the tuna and season with
pepper. Add the tuna and spoon the marinade
over it. Cover with plastic wrap and let marinate
in the refrigerator for 2 hours, turning the
tuna occasionally. Remove the bowl from the
refrigerator about 20 minutes before cooking
to return the fish to room temperature.

2 Remove the tuna from the marinade,
reserving the marinade, and wipe dry. Heat the
remaining oil in a large skillet over high heat.
Add the tuna and sear for 1 minute on each
side until lightly browned and crisp. Place in a
roasting pan. Cover the pan tightly with foil.

3 Roast in a preheated oven, 425°F/220°C, for
8 minutes for medium-rare and 10 minutes for
medium-well done. Remove from the oven and
set aside to rest for 2 minutes before slicing.

4 Meanwhile, place the marinade in a small
pan over high heat and bring to a rolling boil.
Boil for 2 minutes.

5 Transfer the tuna to a serving platter and
carve into thick slices, which will probably
break into chunks as you cut them. Serve the
sauce separately for spooning over.

charbroiled tuna with chile salsa

ingredients

SERVES 4

4 tuna steaks, about
   6 oz/175 g each
grated rind and juice of 1 lime
2 tbsp olive oil
salt and pepper
green salad, to serve

chile salsa

2 orange bell peppers
1 tbsp olive oil
juice of 1 lime
juice of 1 orange
2–3 fresh red chiles, seeded
   and chopped
pinch of cayenne pepper

method

1 Rinse the tuna thoroughly under cold running water and pat dry with paper towels, then place in a large shallow nonmetallic dish. Sprinkle the lime rind and juice and the oil over the fish. Season with salt and pepper, cover with plastic wrap, and let marinate in the refrigerator for up to 1 hour.

2 Preheat the grill. To make the salsa, brush the bell peppers with the olive oil and cook over hot coals, turning frequently, for 10 minutes, or until the skin is blackened and charred. Remove from the grill and let cool slightly, then peel off the skins and discard the seeds. Place the bell peppers in a food processor with the remaining salsa ingredients and process to a purée. Transfer to a bowl and season with salt and pepper.

3 Cook the tuna over hot coals for 4–5 minutes on each side until golden. Transfer to plates, and serve immediately with the green salad and the salsa.

rice, pasta & noodles

Italy and Spain are bordered by miles of Mediterranean coastline, so it is not surprising that fish features prominently in the culinary tradition of these two countries. In Spain, fish and seafood go into what has almost become the national dish—paella. It is often mixed with meat, usually chicken, but Paella with Mussels & White Wine and Seafood Paella with Lemon & Herbs make the most of the daily catch from the sea. The classic Italian rice dish, risotto—a gloriously creamy, rich delight—also works wonderfully well with fish and seafood. Shrimp & Asparagus Risotto and Saffron & Lemon Risotto are both simple yet sophisticated, and if you really love things in shells, Venetian Seafood Risotto is packed with shrimp, mussels, and clams.

Pasta, another Italian favorite, is also a great partner for fish. Smoked salmon goes especially well—try Fettucine with Smoked Salmon or Linguine with Smoked Salmon & Arugula, both light, delicious recipes. Noodles, the Asian version of pasta, are particularly useful if you have a gluten intolerance—you can choose recipes such as Fish Curry with Rice Noodles, Thai Fisherman's Catch, Malaysian-style Coconut Noodles with Shrimp, and Shrimp Laksa, which have all the satisfying texture of noodles but not a hint of wheat!

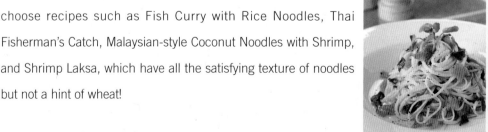

paella with mussels & white wine

ingredients

SERVES 4–6

5¹/₂ oz/150 g cod fillet, skinned
   and rinsed in cold water
44 fl oz/1.35 liters/5¹/₂ cups
   simmering fish stock
7 oz/200 g live mussels,
   prepared (see page 38)
3 tbsp olive oil
1 large red onion, chopped
2 garlic cloves, crushed
¹/₂ tsp cayenne pepper
¹/₂ tsp saffron threads infused
   in 2 tbsp hot water
8 oz/225 g tomatoes, peeled
   and cut into wedges
1 red bell pepper, seeded
   and sliced
1 green bell pepper, seeded
   and sliced
13 oz/375 g/generous
   1¹/₂ cups medium-grain
   paella rice
3¹/₂ fl oz/100 ml/generous
   ¹/₃ cup white wine
5¹/₂ oz/150 g/generous 1 cup
   shelled peas
1 tbsp chopped fresh dill,
   plus extra to garnish
salt and pepper
lemon wedges, to serve

method

1 Cook the cod in the pan of simmering stock for 5 minutes. Transfer to a colander, rinse under cold running water, and drain. Cut into chunks, then transfer to a bowl and set aside. Cook the mussels in the stock for 5 minutes, or until opened, then transfer to the bowl with the cod, discarding any that remain closed.

2 Heat the oil in a paella pan and stir the onion over medium heat until softened. Add the garlic, cayenne pepper, and saffron and its soaking liquid and cook, stirring constantly, for 1 minute. Add the tomatoes and bell peppers and cook, stirring, for 2 minutes.

3 Add the rice and cook, stirring, for 1 minute. Add the wine and most of the stock and bring to a boil, then let simmer for 10 minutes. Do not stir during cooking, but shake the pan once or twice and when adding ingredients. Add the peas, dill, salt, and pepper. Cook for 10 minutes, or until the rice is almost cooked, adding more stock if necessary. Add the cod and mussels and cook for 3 minutes.

4 When all the liquid has been absorbed and you detect a faint toasty aroma coming from the rice, remove from the heat immediately. Cover with foil and let stand for 5 minutes. Garnish with dill and serve with lemon wedges.

seafood paella with lemon & herbs

ingredients

SERVES 4–6

$^1/_2$ tsp saffron threads

2 tbsp hot water

$5^1/_2$ oz/150 g cod fillet, skinned and rinsed under cold running water

42 fl oz/1.25 liters/$5^1/_2$ cups simmering fish stock

12 large raw shrimp, shelled and deveined

1 lb/450 g raw squid, cleaned and cut into rings or bite-size pieces (or use the same quantity of shucked scallops)

3 tbsp olive oil

1 large red onion, chopped

2 garlic cloves, crushed

1 small fresh red chile, seeded and minced

8 oz/225 g tomatoes, peeled and cut into wedges

13 oz/375 g/generous $1^1/_2$ cups medium-grain paella rice

1 tbsp chopped fresh parsley

2 tsp chopped fresh dill

salt and pepper

1 lemon, cut into halves, to serve

method

1 Put the saffron threads and water in a small bowl and let infuse for a few minutes.

2 Add the cod to the pan of simmering stock and cook for 5 minutes, then transfer to a colander, rinse under cold running water and drain. Add the shrimp and squid to the stock and cook for 2 minutes. Cut the cod into chunks, then transfer with the other seafood to a bowl and set aside. Let the stock simmer.

3 Heat the oil in a paella pan and stir the onion over medium heat until softened. Add the garlic, chile, and saffron and its soaking liquid and cook, stirring, for 1 minute. Add the tomato wedges and cook, stirring, for 2 minutes. Add the rice and herbs and cook, stirring, for 1 minute. Add most of the stock and bring to a boil. Let simmer, uncovered, for 10 minutes. Do not stir during cooking, but shake the pan once or twice and when adding ingredients. Season and cook for 10 minutes, until the rice is almost cooked. Add more stock if necessary. Add the seafood and cook for 2 minutes.

4 When all the liquid has been absorbed and you detect a faint toasty aroma coming from the rice, remove from the heat immediately. Cover with foil and let stand for 5 minutes. Serve with the lemon halves.

risotto with tuna & pine nuts

ingredients

SERVES 4

3 tbsp butter

4 tbsp olive oil

1 small onion, finely chopped

10 oz/280 g/1^{1}/$_{2}$ cups
Arborio rice

40 fl oz/1.25 liters/5 cups
simmering fish or chicken
stock

salt and pepper

8 oz/225 g tuna, canned
and drained, or broiled
fresh steaks

8–10 black olives, pitted
and sliced

1 small pimiento, thinly sliced

1 tsp finely chopped
fresh parsley

1 tsp finely chopped
fresh marjoram

2 tbsp white wine vinegar

2 oz/55 g/^{3}/$_{8}$ cup pine nuts

1 garlic clove, chopped

8 oz/225 g fresh tomatoes,
peeled, seeded, and diced

3 oz/85 g/^{3}/$_{4}$ cup Parmesan
or Grana Padano cheese

method

1 Melt 2 tablespoons of the butter with 1 tablespoon of the oil in a deep pan over medium heat. Add the onion and cook, stirring occasionally, until soft and starting to turn golden. Reduce the heat, add the rice, and mix to coat in oil and butter. Cook, stirring constantly, until the grains are translucent. Add the hot stock, a ladleful at a time, stirring constantly, until all the liquid is absorbed and the rice is creamy. Season to taste.

2 While the risotto is cooking, flake the tuna into a bowl and mix in the olives, pimiento, parsley, marjoram, and vinegar. Season with salt and pepper.

3 Heat the remaining oil in a small skillet over high heat. Add the pine nuts and garlic. Cook, stirring constantly, for 2 minutes, or until they just start to brown. Add the tomatoes and mix well. Continue cooking over medium heat for 3–4 minutes or until they are thoroughly warm. Pour the tomato mixture over the tuna mixture and mix. Fold into the risotto 5 minutes before the end of the cooking time.

4 Remove the risotto from the heat when all the liquid has been absorbed and add the remaining butter. Mix well, then stir in the Parmesan until it melts. Serve at once.

risotto with sole & tomatoes

ingredients

SERVES 4

3 tbsp butter

3 tbsp olive oil

1 small onion, finely chopped

10 oz/280 g/1½ cups
   Arborio rice

40 fl oz/1.25 liters/5 cups
   simmering fish or chicken
   stock

salt and pepper

1 lb/450 g tomatoes, peeled,
   seeded, and cut into strips

6 sun-dried tomatoes in olive
   oil, drained and thinly sliced

3 tbsp tomato paste

2 fl oz/50 ml/¼ cup red wine

1 lb/450 g sole or flounder
   fillets, skinned

4 oz/115 g/1 cup freshly
   grated Parmesan or Grana
   Padano cheese

2 tbsp finely chopped fresh
   cilantro, to garnish

method

1 Melt 2 tablespoons of the butter with
1 tablespoon of the oil in a deep pan over
medium heat. Stir in the onion and cook, stirring
occasionally, for 5 minutes, or until soft and
starting to turn golden. Reduce the heat, add
the rice, and mix to coat in oil and butter.
Cook, stirring constantly, for 2–3 minutes, or
until the grains are translucent. Add the hot
stock, a ladleful at a time, stirring constantly,
until all the liquid is absorbed and the rice is
creamy. Season with salt and pepper.

2 Meanwhile, heat the remaining oil in a large,
heavy-bottom skillet. Add the fresh and dried
tomatoes. Stir well and cook over medium
heat for 10–15 minutes, or until soft and
slushy. Stir in the tomato paste and wine.
Bring to a boil, then reduce the heat until it is
just simmering. Cut the fish into strips and
gently stir into the sauce. Cook for 5 minutes,
or until the fish flakes when checked with a
fork. Most of the liquid should be absorbed
but, if it isn't, remove the fish and then
increase the heat to reduce the sauce.

3 Remove the risotto from the heat when
all the liquid has been absorbed and add the
remaining butter. Mix well, then stir in the
Parmesan until it melts. Place the risotto on
serving plates and arrange the fish and sauce
on top. Garnish with chopped fresh cilantro
and serve at once.

venetian seafood risotto

ingredients

SERVES 4

8 oz/225 g prepared raw
   shrimp, heads and
   shells reserved

2 garlic cloves, halved

1 lemon, sliced

8 oz/225 g live mussels*,
   scrubbed and debearded

8 oz/225 g live clams*,
   scrubbed

20 fl oz/625 ml/2^1/$_2$ cups
   water

4 oz/115 g butter

1 tbsp olive oil

1 onion, finely chopped

2 tbsp chopped fresh
   flat-leaf parsley

12 oz/350 g/1^3/$_4$ cups
   Arborio rice

4 fl oz/125 ml/^{1}/$_2$ cup
   dry white wine

8 oz/225 g cleaned raw
   squid, cut into small
   pieces, or squid rings

4 tbsp Marsala

salt and pepper

* discard any mussels or
clams that remain closed
after cooking

method

1 Wrap the shrimp heads and shells in a square of cheesecloth and pound with a pestle. Put the wrapped shells and their liquid in a pan with the garlic, lemon, mussels, and clams. Add the measured water, cover, and bring to a boil over high heat. Cook, shaking the pan frequently, for 5 minutes until the shellfish have opened. Let cool, shell and set aside. Strain the cooking liquid through a strainer lined with cheesecloth and add water to make 40 fl oz/1.25 liters/5 cups. Bring to a boil in a pan, then simmer gently over low heat.

2 Melt 2 tablespoons of butter with the olive oil in a pan. Cook the onion and half the parsley over medium heat, stirring occasionally, until softened. Reduce the heat, stir in the rice, and cook, stirring, until the grains are translucent. Add the wine and cook, stirring, for 1 minute until reduced. Add the hot cooking liquid a ladleful at a time, stirring constantly, until all the liquid is absorbed and the rice is creamy.

3 Melt 2 oz/55 g of the remaining butter in a pan. Cook the squid, stirring frequently, for 3 minutes. Add the shrimp and cook for 2–3 minutes, until the squid is opaque and the shrimp have changed color. Add the Marsala, bring to a boil, and cook until the liquid has evaporated. Stir all the seafood into the rice, add the remaining butter and parsley, and season. Heat gently and serve at once.

lobster risotto

ingredients

SERVES 2

1 cooked lobster, about
  14 oz–1 lb/400–450 g
1 tbsp olive oil
2 oz/55 g butter
$^1/_2$ onion, finely chopped
1 garlic clove, finely chopped
1 tsp chopped fresh thyme
  leaves
6 oz/175 g/generous $^3/_4$ cup
  Arborio rice
5 fl oz/150 ml/$^2/_3$ cup
  sparkling white wine
20 fl oz/625 ml/2$^1/_2$ cups
  simmering fish stock
1 tsp green or pink
  peppercorns in brine,
  drained and coarsely
  chopped
1 tbsp chopped fresh parsley

method

1 To prepare the lobster, remove the claws by twisting them. Crack the claws using the back of a large knife and set aside. Split the body lengthwise. Remove and discard the intestinal vein, the stomach sac, and the spongy gills. Remove the meat from the tail and coarsely chop. Set aside with the claws.

2 Heat the oil with half the butter in a large pan over medium heat. Add the onion and cook, stirring occasionally, for 5 minutes until softened. Add the garlic and cook for an additional 30 seconds. Stir in the thyme. Reduce the heat, add the rice, and mix to coat in butter and oil. Cook, stirring constantly, for 2–3 minutes, or until the grains are translucent.

3 Stir in the wine and cook, stirring constantly, for 1 minute until reduced. Gradually add the hot stock, a ladleful at a time. Stir constantly and add more liquid as the rice absorbs each addition. Increase the heat to medium so that the liquid bubbles. Cook for 20 minutes, or until all the liquid is absorbed and the rice is creamy. Five minutes before the end of cooking time, add the lobster meat and claws.

4 Remove the pan from the heat and stir in the peppercorns, remaining butter, and the parsley. Spoon on to warmed plates and serve at once.

shrimp & asparagus risotto

ingredients

SERVES 4

40 fl oz/1.25 liters/5 cups
   vegetable stock
12 oz/375 g fresh asparagus
   spears, cut into 2-inch/
   5-cm lengths
2 tbsp olive oil
1 onion, finely chopped
1 garlic clove, finely chopped
12 oz/350 g/1³/₄ cups
   Arborio rice
1 lb/450 g raw jumbo shrimp,
   shelled and deveined
2 tbsp olive paste or tapenade
2 tbsp chopped fresh basil
salt and pepper
fresh Parmesan cheese and
   fresh basil sprigs,
   to garnish

method

1 Bring the stock to a boil in a large pan. Add the asparagus and cook for 3 minutes until just tender. Strain, reserving the stock, and refresh the asparagus under cold running water. Drain and set aside. Return the stock to the pan and keep simmering gently over low heat while you are cooking the risotto.

2 Heat the olive oil in a large, heavy-bottom pan. Add the onion and cook over medium heat, stirring occasionally, for 5 minutes until softened. Add the garlic and cook for an additional 30 seconds. Reduce the heat, add the rice, and mix to coat in oil. Cook, stirring constantly, for 2–3 minutes, or until the grains are translucent.

3 Gradually add the hot stock, a ladleful at a time. Stir constantly and add more liquid as the rice absorbs each addition. Increase the heat to medium so that the liquid bubbles. Cook for 20 minutes, until all the liquid is absorbed and the rice is creamy. Add the shrimp and asparagus when you add the last ladleful of stock.

4 Remove the pan from the heat, stir in the olive paste and basil, and season with salt and pepper. Spoon the risotto onto warmed plates and serve at once, garnished with Parmesan cheese and basil sprigs.

saffron & lemon risotto with scallops

ingredients

SERVES 4

16 live scallops, shucked

juice of 1 lemon, plus extra
for seasoning

3 tbsp butter

1 tbsp olive oil, plus extra for
brushing

1 small onion, finely chopped

10 oz/280 g/1¹/2 cups
Arborio rice

1 tsp crumbled saffron
threads

40 fl oz/1.25 liters/5 cups
simmering fish or
vegetable stock

salt and pepper

2 tbsp vegetable oil

4 oz/115 g/1 cup freshly
grated Parmesan or Grana
Padano cheese

1 lemon, cut into wedges and
2 tsp lemon zest, to
garnish

method

1 Place the scallops in a nonmetallic bowl and mix with the lemon juice. Cover the bowl with plastic wrap and let chill for 15 minutes.

2 Melt 2 tablespoons of the butter with the oil in a deep pan over medium heat. Add the onion and cook, stirring occasionally, until soft and starting to turn golden. Add the rice and mix to coat in oil and butter. Cook, stirring, until the grains are translucent. Dissolve the saffron in 4 tablespoons of hot stock and add to the rice. Gradually add the remaining stock a ladleful at a time, stirring constantly, until all the liquid is absorbed and the rice is creamy. Season with salt and pepper.

3 When the risotto is nearly cooked, preheat a grill pan over high heat. Brush the scallops with oil and sear on the grill pan for 3–4 minutes on each side, depending on their thickness. Take care not to overcook or they will be rubbery.

4 Remove the risotto from the heat and add the remaining butter. Mix well, then stir in the Parmesan until it melts. Season with lemon juice, adding just 1 teaspoon at a time and tasting as you go. Serve the risotto at once with the scallops and lemon wedges arranged on top, sprinkled with lemon zest.

risotto with squid & garlic butter

ingredients

SERVES 4

8–12 raw baby squid,
cleaned, rinsed, and
patted dry

5^1/$_2$ oz/150 g butter

1 tbsp olive oil

1 small onion, finely chopped

10 oz/280 g/scant 1^1/$_2$ cups
Arborio rice

40 fl oz/1.25 liters/5 cups
simmering fish
or chicken stock

salt and pepper

3 garlic cloves, crushed

3 oz/85 g/^{3}/$_4$ cup freshly
grated Parmesan or Grana
Padano cheese

2 tbsp finely chopped fresh
parsley, to garnish

method

1 Cut the squid in half lengthwise, then score with a sharp knife, making horizontal and vertical cuts. Dice the larger tentacles.

2 Melt 2 tablespoons of the butter with the oil in a deep pan over medium heat. Cook the onion, stirring, until soft and starting to turn golden. Stir in the rice and cook, stirring, until the grains are translucent. Gradually add the hot stock, a ladleful at a time. Stir constantly and add more liquid as the rice absorbs each addition. Cook for 20 minutes, or until all the liquid is absorbed and the rice is creamy. Season with salt and pepper.

3 When the risotto is nearly cooked, melt 4 oz/ 115 g of the remaining butter in a heavy-bottom skillet. Add the garlic and cook over low heat until soft. Increase the heat to high, add the squid, and toss to cook for no more than 2–3 minutes or the squid will become tough. Remove the squid from the skillet, draining carefully and reserving the garlic butter.

4 Remove the risotto from the heat and stir in the remaining butter, then stir in the Parmesan until it melts. Spoon onto warmed serving plates and arrange the squid on top. Spoon some of the garlic butter over each portion. Serve at once, sprinkled with chopped parsley.

shrimp with coconut rice

ingredients

SERVES 4

4 oz/115 g/1 cup dried
  Chinese mushrooms

2 tbsp vegetable or
  peanut oil

6 scallions, chopped

2 oz/55 g/scant $^1\!/_2$ cup dry
  unsweetened coconut

1 fresh green chile, seeded
  and chopped

8 oz/225 g/generous 1 cup
  jasmine rice

5 fl oz/150 ml/$^2\!/_3$ cup
  fish stock

14 fl oz/425 ml/1$^3\!/_4$ cups
  coconut milk

12 oz/350 g cooked shelled
  shrimp

6 sprigs fresh Thai basil

method

1 Place the mushrooms in a small bowl, cover with hot water, and set aside to soak for 30 minutes. Drain, then cut off and discard the stalks and slice the caps.

2 Heat 1 tablespoon of the oil in a wok and stir-fry the scallions, coconut, and chile for 2–3 minutes, until lightly browned. Add the mushrooms and stir-fry for 3–4 minutes.

3 Add the rice and stir-fry for 2–3 minutes, then add the stock and bring to a boil. Reduce the heat and add the coconut milk. Let simmer for 10–15 minutes, until the rice is tender. Stir in the shrimp and basil, heat through, and serve.

smoked fish with tagliatelle verde

ingredients

SERVES 4

1 lb/450 g smoked haddock
   fillets, skinned
10 oz/280 g dried tagliatelle
   verde
20 fl oz/625 ml/2$^1/_2$ cups
   skim or lowfat milk
4 tbsp cornstarch
2 shallots, finely chopped
2 tbsp snipped fresh chives
pepper

method

1 Cut the fish into chunks, removing any remaining bones.

2 Bring a large pan of water to a boil, add the tagliatelle, and return to a boil. Cook for 8–10 minutes, or until just tender.

3 Meanwhile, blend 4 fl oz/125 ml/$^1/_2$ cup of the milk with the cornstarch in a heatproof 28-fl oz/875-ml/3$^1/_2$-cup bowl. Place the remaining milk in a pan with the shallots and bring to a boil. Pour the boiling milk over the cornstarch mixture, stirring constantly. Return the milk to the pan and return to a boil, stirring constantly, until the sauce thickens.

4 Stir the fish into the sauce, reduce the heat to low, and let simmer gently for 5 minutes, or until the fish is cooked. Stir in half of the chives.

5 Drain the tagliatelle and return to the pan, stir in the haddock sauce, and season with pepper. Serve at once, garnished with the remaining chives.

fettuccine with smoked salmon

ingredients

SERVES 4

8 oz/225 g dried fettuccine

1 tsp olive oil

1 garlic clove, finely chopped

2 oz/55 g smoked salmon,
    cut into thin strips

2 oz/55 g watercress leaves,
    plus extra to garnish

salt and pepper

method

1 Bring a large pan of lightly salted water to a boil over medium heat. Add the pasta, return to a boil and cook for 8–10 minutes, or until tender but still firm to the bite.

2 Meanwhile, heat the olive oil in a large nonstick skillet. Add the garlic and cook over low heat, stirring constantly, for 30 seconds. Add the salmon and watercress, season with pepper, and cook for an additional 30 seconds, or until the watercress has wilted.

3 Drain the cooked pasta and return to the pan. Mix the salmon and watercress with the pasta. Toss the mixture thoroughly using 2 large forks. Divide among 4 large serving plates and garnish with extra watercress leaves. Serve immediately.

linguine with smoked salmon & arugula

ingredients

SERVES 4

12 oz/350 g dried linguine

2 tbsp olive oil

1 garlic clove, finely chopped

4 oz/115 g smoked salmon,
    cut into thin strips

2 oz/55 g arugula

salt and pepper

lemon halves, to garnish

method

1 Bring a large, heavy-bottom pan of lightly salted water to a boil. Add the pasta, return to a boil, and cook for 8–10 minutes, or until tender but still firm to the bite.

2 Just before the end of the cooking time, heat the olive oil in a heavy-bottom skillet. Add the garlic and cook over low heat, stirring constantly, for 1 minute. Do not allow the garlic to brown or it will taste bitter. Add the salmon and arugula. Season with salt and pepper and cook, stirring constantly, for 1 minute. Remove the skillet from the heat.

3 Drain the pasta and transfer to a warmed serving dish. Add the smoked salmon and arugula mixture, toss lightly, and serve, garnished with lemon halves.

macaroni & seafood bake

ingredients

SERVES 4

12 oz/350 g dried
short-cut macaroni
6 tbsp butter, plus extra for
greasing
2 small fennel bulbs,
thinly sliced
6 oz/175 g mushrooms,
thinly sliced
6 oz/175 g cooked
shelled shrimp
pinch of cayenne pepper
1¼ cups Béchamel Sauce
(see below)
½ cup freshly grated
Parmesan cheese
2 large tomatoes, sliced
olive oil, for brushing
1 tsp dried oregano
salt and pepper

béchamel sauce

10 fl oz/300 ml/1¼ cups milk
1 bay leaf
6 black peppercorns
slice of onion
mace blade
2 tbsp butter
3 tbsp all-purpose flour
salt and pepper

method

1 To make the Béchamel sauce, pour the milk into a pan and add the bay leaf, peppercorns, onion, and mace. Heat to just below boiling point, then remove from the heat, cover, let infuse for 10 minutes, then strain. Melt the butter in a separate pan. Sprinkle in the flour and cook over low heat, stirring constantly, for 1 minute. Gradually stir in the milk, then bring to a boil and cook, stirring, until thickened and smooth. Season with salt and pepper.

2 Bring a large pan of lightly salted water to a boil. Add the pasta, return to a boil, and cook for 8–10 minutes, or until tender but still firm to the bite. Drain and return to the pan. Add 2 tablespoons of the butter to the pasta, cover, shake the pan, and keep warm.

3 Melt the remaining butter in a pan. Add the fennel and cook for 3–4 minutes. Stir in the mushrooms and cook for 2 minutes. Stir in the shrimp, then remove the pan from the heat. Stir the cayenne pepper into the Béchamel sauce and add the shrimp mixture and pasta.

4 Grease a large ovenproof dish with butter, then pour the mixture into the dish and spread evenly. Sprinkle over the Parmesan cheese and arrange the tomato slices in a ring around the edge. Brush the tomatoes with olive oil, then sprinkle over the oregano. Bake in a preheated oven, 350°F/180°C, for 25 minutes, or until golden brown. Serve immediately.

crab ravioli

ingredients

SERVES 4

6 scallions

12 oz/350 g cooked crabmeat

2 tsp finely chopped
   fresh gingerroot

1/8–1/4 tsp chili or Tabasco
   sauce

1 lb 9 oz/700 g tomatoes,
   peeled, seeded, and
   coarsely chopped

1 garlic clove, finely chopped

1 tbsp white wine vinegar

1 quantity basic pasta dough
   (see below)

all-purpose flour, for dusting

1 egg, lightly beaten

salt

2 tbsp heavy cream

shredded scallion, to garnish

pasta dough

7 oz/200 g/1 cup all-purpose
   flour, plus extra for dusting

pinch of salt

2 eggs, lightly beaten

1 tbsp olive oil

method

1 To make the pasta dough, sift the flour into a food processor. Add the salt, eggs, and olive oil and process until the dough begins to come together. Knead on a lightly floured counter until smooth. Cover and let rest for 30 minutes.

2 Thinly slice the scallions, keeping the white and green parts separate. Mix the green scallions, crabmeat, gingerroot, and chili sauce to taste in a bowl. Cover and let chill.

3 Process the tomatoes in a food processor to a purée. Place the garlic, white scallions, and vinegar in a pan and add the puréed tomatoes. Bring to a boil, stirring, then let simmer gently for 10 minutes. Remove from the heat.

4 Thinly roll out half of the pasta dough on a lightly floured counter. Cover with a dish towel and roll out the other half. Place small mounds of the filling in rows 1 1/2 inches/4 cm apart on one sheet of dough and brush in between with beaten egg. Cover with the other half of dough. Press down between the mounds, cut into squares, and let rest on a dish towel for 1 hour.

5 Bring a large pan of lightly salted water to a boil. Add the ravioli, in batches, return to a boil, and cook for 5 minutes. Remove with a slotted spoon and drain on paper towels. Meanwhile, gently heat the tomato sauce and whisk in the cream. Serve the ravioli with the sauce poured over and garnished with shredded scallion.

spaghetti with clams

ingredients

SERVES 4

2 lb 4 oz/1 kg live clams,
    scrubbed under cold
    running water*
6 fl oz/175 ml/³/4 cup water
6 fl oz/175 ml/³/4 cup dry
    white wine
12 oz/350 g dried spaghetti
5 tbsp olive oil
2 garlic cloves, finely chopped
4 tbsp chopped fresh
    flat-leaf parsley
salt and pepper

* discard any clams with
broken or damaged shells
and any that do not shut
when sharply tapped

method

1 Place the clams in a large, heavy-bottom pan, add the water and wine, cover, and cook over high heat, shaking the pan occasionally, for 5 minutes, or until the shells have opened.

2 Remove the clams with a slotted spoon and let cool slightly. Strain the cooking liquid into a small pan through a strainer lined with cheesecloth. Bring to a boil and cook until reduced by about half, then remove from the heat. Meanwhile, discard any clams that have not opened, remove the remainder from their shells, and reserve until required.

3 Bring a large pan of lightly salted water to a boil. Add the pasta, return to a boil, and cook for 8–10 minutes, or until tender but still firm to the bite.

4 Meanwhile, heat the olive oil in a large, heavy-bottom skillet. Add the garlic and cook, stirring frequently, for 2 minutes. Add the parsley and the reduced clam cooking liquid and let simmer gently.

5 Drain the pasta and add it to the skillet with the clams. Season with salt and pepper and cook, stirring constantly, for 4 minutes, or until the pasta is coated and the clams have heated through. Transfer to a warmed serving dish and serve immediately.

fish curry with rice noodles

ingredients

SERVES 4

2 tbsp vegetable or peanut oil

1 large onion, chopped

2 garlic cloves, chopped

3 oz/85 g white mushrooms

8 oz/225 g monkfish, cut into
   1-inch/2.5-cm cubes

8 oz/225 g salmon fillets, cut
   into 1-inch/2.5-cm cubes

8 oz/225 g cod fillets, cut into
   1-inch/2.5-cm cubes

2 tbsp Thai red curry paste

14 oz/400 g/1$\frac{3}{4}$ cups canned
   coconut milk

handful of fresh cilantro,
   chopped

1 tsp jaggery or brown sugar

1 tsp Thai fish sauce

4 oz/115 g dried rice noodles

3 scallions, chopped

2 oz/50 g/scant $\frac{1}{2}$ cup bean
   sprouts

few fresh Thai basil leaves

method

1 Heat the oil in a preheated wok or large skillet over medium heat, add the onion, garlic, and mushrooms and cook, stirring frequently, for 5 minutes until softened, but not browned.

2 Add the fish, curry paste, and coconut milk and bring gently to a boil. Let simmer for 2–3 minutes before adding half the cilantro, and the sugar and fish sauce. Keep warm.

3 Meanwhile, soak the noodles in enough boiling water to cover in a heatproof bowl for 3–4 minutes until tender, or cook according to the package instructions. Drain well through a metal colander. Put the colander and noodles over a pan of simmering water. Add the scallions, bean sprouts, and most of the basil and steam on top of the noodles for 1–2 minutes until just wilted.

4 Pile the noodles onto warmed serving plates and top with the fish curry. Sprinkle the remaining cilantro and basil over the top and serve at once.

cod with spiced noodles

ingredients

SERVES 4

1 tbsp peanut or corn oil

finely grated rind and juice of
    1 large lemon

4 cod or haddock steaks,
    about 5 oz/140 g each,
    skinned

paprika, to taste

salt and pepper

spiced noodles

9 oz/250 g dried medium
    Chinese egg noodles

1 tbsp peanut or corn oil

2 garlic cloves, chopped

1-inch/2.5-cm piece fresh
    gingerroot, peeled and
    finely chopped

2 tbsp very finely chopped
    fresh cilantro roots

1 tbsp kecap manis (sweet
    soy sauce)

1 Thai chile, seeded and
    finely chopped

1 tbsp nam pla
    (Thai fish sauce)

method

1 Put the noodles in a pan of boiling water and boil for 3 minutes, until soft, or cook according to the package instructions. Drain, rinse with cold water to stop the cooking, and drain again, then set aside.

2 Mix 1 tablespoon of the oil with the lemon juice and brush over one side of each fish steak. Sprinkle with the lemon rind and a dusting of paprika and add a little salt and pepper. Lightly brush a broiler rack with oil, then place the fish on the rack and broil under a broiler preheated to high, about 4 inches/ 10 cm from the heat, for 8–10 minutes, until the flesh flakes easily.

3 Meanwhile, heat a wok or large skillet over high heat. Add 1 tablespoon oil and heat until it shimmers. Add the garlic and gingerroot and stir-fry for about 30 seconds. Add the cilantro and kecap manis and stir round. Add the noodles and stir thoroughly so they are coated in the kecap manis. Stir in the chopped chile and nam pla. Serve each broiled fish steak on a bed of noodles.

teriyaki salmon fillets with chinese noodles

ingredients

SERVES 4

4 salmon fillets, about
    7 oz/200 g each, any
    scales wiped off
4 fl oz/125 ml/^{1}/$_2$ cup
    teriyaki marinade
1 shallot, sliced
^{3}/$_4$-inch/2-cm piece fresh
    gingerroot, finely chopped
2 carrots, sliced
4 oz/115 g closed-cup
    mushrooms, sliced
40 fl oz/1.25 liters/5 cups
    vegetable stock
9 oz/250 g dried medium egg
    noodles
4 oz/115 g/1 cup frozen peas
6 oz/175 g Napa cabbage,
    shredded
4 scallions, sliced

method

1 Arrange the salmon fillets, skin-side up, in a dish just large enough to fit them in a single layer. Mix the teriyaki marinade with the shallot and gingerroot and pour over the fish. Cover and let marinate in the refrigerator for 1 hour, turning the salmon over once.

2 Put the carrots, mushrooms, and stock into a large pan. Arrange the salmon, skin-side down, on a shallow cookie sheet. Pour the fish marinade into the pan of vegetables and stock and bring to a boil. Reduce the heat, cover, and let simmer for 10 minutes.

3 Meanwhile, cook the salmon under a broiler preheated to medium for 10–15 minutes, until the flesh turns pink and flakes easily. Remove from the broiler and keep warm.

4 Add the noodles and peas to the stock and return to a boil. Reduce the heat, cover, and let simmer for 5 minutes, or until the noodles are tender. Stir in the Napa cabbage and scallions and heat through for 1 minute.

5 Drain off 10 fl oz/300 ml/1^1/$_4$ cups of the stock into a heatproof pitcher and set aside. Drain and discard the remaining stock. Divide the noodles and vegetables among 4 warmed serving bowls and top each with a salmon fillet. Pour over the reserved stock and serve.

thai fisherman's catch

ingredients

SERVES 4

20 cooked jumbo shrimp

20 cooked mussels in their
shells*

2 oz/55 g oyster mushrooms,
wiped

2 scallions, finely sliced

3 kaffir lime leaves,
thinly sliced

1 lemongrass stalk, center
part only, finely chopped

1/2 red onion, very thinly sliced

3 1/2 oz/100 g dried medium
rice noodles

thai coconut dressing

4 fl oz/125 ml/1/2 cup
creamed coconut

3 tbsp lime juice

1 1/2 tbsp nam pla (Thai fish
sauce)

1 1/2 tbsp brown sugar

1–2 fresh red chiles, to taste,
seeded and thinly sliced

1 small garlic clove, crushed

* discard any mussels that
remain closed after cooking

method

1 To make the dressing, stir all the ingredients together in a large bowl until the sugar dissolves. Add the shrimp, mussels, mushrooms, scallions, lime leaves, lemongrass, and red onion, then cover and let chill until required.

2 Meanwhile, soak the noodles in a bowl with enough lukewarm water to cover for 20 minutes, until soft, or cook according to the package instructions. Drain well.

3 To serve, divide the noodles among 4 bowls. Spoon the seafood salad over them, adding any extra dressing.

malaysian-style coconut noodles with shrimp

ingredients

SERVES 4

2 tbsp vegetable oil

1 small red bell pepper, seeded and diced

7 oz/200 g bok choy, stalks thinly sliced and leaves chopped

2 large garlic cloves, chopped

1 tsp ground turmeric

2 tsp garam masala

1 tsp chili powder (optional)

4 fl oz/125 ml/1/2 cup hot vegetable stock

2 heaping tbsp smooth peanut butter

12 oz/350 ml/1 1/2 cups coconut milk

1 tbsp soy sauce

9 oz/250 g thick rice noodles

10 oz/280 g cooked shelled jumbo shrimp

2 scallions, finely shredded and 1 tbsp sesame seeds, to garnish

method

1 Heat the oil in a preheated wok or large, heavy-bottom skillet over high heat. Add the red bell pepper, bok choy stalks, and garlic and stir-fry for 3 minutes. Add the turmeric, garam masala, chili powder, if using, and bok choy leaves, and stir-fry for 1 minute.

2 Mix the hot stock and peanut butter together in a heatproof bowl until the peanut butter has dissolved, then add to the stir-fry with the coconut milk and tamari. Cook for 5 minutes over medium heat, or until reduced and thickened.

3 Meanwhile, immerse the noodles in a bowl of just boiled water. Let stand for 4 minutes, then drain and refresh the noodles under cold running water. Add the cooked noodles and shrimp to the coconut curry and cook for an additional 2–3 minutes, stirring frequently, until heated through.

4 Serve the noodle dish sprinkled with scallions and sesame seeds.

shrimp laksa

ingredients

SERVES 4

20–24 large raw unshelled
 shrimp
16 fl oz/450 ml/2 cups
 fish stock
pinch of salt
16 fl oz/450 ml/2 cups
 coconut milk
2 tsp nam pla (Thai fish sauce)
$1/2$ tablespoon lime juice
4 oz/115 g dried medium
 rice-flour noodles
4 oz/115 g/$1/2$ cup
 bean sprouts
fresh cilantro, chopped,
 to garnish

laksa paste

6 fresh cilantro stalks with
 leaves
3 large garlic cloves, crushed
1 fresh red chile, seeded and
 chopped
1 lemongrass stalk, center
 part only, chopped
1-inch/2.5-cm piece fresh
 gingerroot, peeled and
 chopped
$1^1/2$ tbsp shrimp paste
$1/2$ tsp ground turmeric
peanut oil

method

1 Remove the heads and shells from the shrimp, leaving the tails intact, and devein. Reserve the heads and shells. Put the fish stock, salt, and the shrimp heads and shells in a pan over high heat and slowly bring to a boil. Lower the heat and let simmer for 10 minutes.

2 Meanwhile, make the laksa paste. Put all the ingredients, except the oil, in a food processor and blend. With the motor running, slowly add up to 2 tablespoons of peanut oil just until a paste forms. (If your food processor is too large to work efficiently with this small quantity, use a mortar and pestle.)

3 Heat 1 teaspoon of peanut oil in a large pan over high heat. Add the paste and stir-fry until it is fragrant. Strain the fish stock through a strainer lined with cheesecloth. Stir the stock into the laksa paste, along with the coconut milk, nam pla, and lime juice. Bring to a boil, then cover and let simmer for 30 minutes.

4 Meanwhile, soak the noodles in a large bowl with enough lukewarm water to cover for 20 minutes, until soft. Drain and set aside.

5 Add the shrimp and bean sprouts to the soup and continue simmering just until the shrimp turn opaque and curl. Divide the noodles among 4 bowls and ladle the soup over. Garnish with chopped cilantro and serve.

scallops on noodles

ingredients

SERVES 4

4 oz/115 g dried green tea
   noodles, or the thinnest
   green noodles you can find

1 oz/30 g butter

1 garlic clove, crushed

pinch of paprika

1 tbsp peanut or corn oil, plus
   a little extra for cooking
   the scallops

2 tbsp bottled mild or medium
   Thai green curry paste

2 tbsp water

2 tsp light soy sauce

2 scallions, finely shredded,
   and extra scallions, sliced,
   to garnish

12 fresh scallops, shucked,
   with shells reserved, if
   possible

salt and pepper

method

1 Boil the green tea noodles for about 1$^{1}/_{2}$ minutes, until soft, then rinse with cold water and drain well. For any other noodles, follow the package instructions. Drain and set aside. Meanwhile, melt the butter in a small pan and cook the garlic in it for about 1 minute. Add the paprika and set aside.

2 Heat a wok over high heat. Add the oil. Stir in the curry paste, water, and soy sauce and bring to a boil. Add the noodles and stir around to reheat. Stir in the scallions, then remove from the heat and keep warm.

3 Heat a ridged, cast-iron grill pan over high heat and brush lightly with a little oil. Add the scallops to the pan and cook for 3 minutes on the first side, then no more than 2 minutes on the second, brushing with the garlic butter, until just cooked (the center shouldn't be totally opaque if cut open). Season with salt and pepper. Divide the noodles among 4 serving plates and top with 3 scallops each. Garnish with spring onions and serve immediately.

salads & stir-fries

Salads and stir-fries are two of the most healthy ways to eat vegetables, and adding a first-class protein in the form of fish and seafood makes an ideal combination. This chapter is filled with inspiring ideas for those who have health problems, or who believe that prevention is better than cure!

Salmon & Avocado Salad, Smoked Salmon, Asparagus & Avocado Salad, Tuna & Two-bean Salad, Shrimp & Papaya Salad, and Monkfish Stir-fry are excellent options for maintaining a healthy heart, and diabetics can enjoy Tuna & Avocado Salad and Coconut Shrimp with Cucumber Salad. Avocado, rather like oil-rich fish, is often viewed with suspicion because of its high fat content, but the fat is almost entirely monounsaturated and is excellent for the circulatory system. It also has a fabulous, smooth texture that goes very well with fresh or smoked salmon and fresh tuna, so recipes with these ingredients have a recklessly indulgent air about them and feed the soul as well as the body!

If you are not on a restricted diet and simply love salads and stir-fries, Smoked Salmon & Wild Arugula Salad has an irresistible lime-mayonnaise dressing, and Salmon & Scallops with Cilantro & Lime is packed with flavor for a special occasion.

salmon & avocado salad

ingredients

SERVES 4

1 lb/450 g new potatoes

4 salmon steaks, about
4 oz/115 g each

1 avocado

juice of $\frac{1}{2}$ lemon

2 oz/55 g baby spinach
leaves

$4\frac{1}{2}$ oz/125 g mixed small
salad greens, including
watercress

4 tomatoes, cut into fourths

2 oz/55 g/scant $\frac{1}{2}$ cup
chopped walnuts

dressing

3 tbsp unsweetened clear
apple juice

1 tsp balsamic vinegar

pepper

method

1 Cut the new potatoes into bite-size pieces, put into a pan, and cover with cold water. Bring to a boil, then reduce the heat, cover, and let simmer for 10–15 minutes, or until just tender. Drain and keep warm.

2 Meanwhile, preheat the broiler to medium. Cook the salmon steaks under the preheated broiler for 10–15 minutes, depending on the thickness of the steaks, turning halfway through cooking. Remove from the broiler and keep warm.

3 While the potatoes and salmon are cooking, cut the avocado in half, remove and discard the pit, and peel the flesh. Cut the avocado flesh into slices and coat in the lemon juice to prevent discoloration.

4 Toss the spinach leaves and mixed salad greens together in a large serving bowl until combined. Arrange the greens and the tomato fourths on individual serving plates.

5 Remove and discard the skin and any bones from the salmon. Flake the salmon and divide among the plates along with the potatoes. Sprinkle the walnuts over the salads.

6 To make the dressing, mix the apple juice and vinegar together in a small bowl or pitcher and season well with pepper. Drizzle over the salads and serve at once.

smoked salmon, asparagus & avocado salad

ingredients

SERVES 4

7 oz/200 g asparagus spears
1 large avocado
1 tbsp lemon juice
large handful of arugula leaves
8 oz/225 g smoked salmon
1 red onion, finely sliced
1 tbsp chopped fresh flat-leaf
   parsley, plus extra sprigs
   to garnish
1 tbsp snipped fresh chives
lemon wedges, to garnish
whole wheat bread, to serve

dressing

1 garlic clove, chopped
4 tbsp extra-virgin olive oil
2 tbsp white wine vinegar
1 tbsp lemon juice
pinch of sugar
1 tsp mustard

method

1 Bring a large pan of salted water to a boil, add the asparagus, and blanch for 4 minutes. Drain and plunge into cold water, then drain again. Set aside to cool.

2 To make the dressing, combine all the dressing ingredients in a small bowl and stir together well.

3 Halve, peel, and pit the avocado and cut into bite-size pieces. Brush with the lemon juice to prevent discoloration.

4 To assemble the salad, arrange the arugula leaves on individual serving plates and top with the asparagus and avocado. Cut the smoked salmon into strips and arrange over the top of the salads, then sprinkle over the onion and herbs. Drizzle over the dressing, then garnish with parsley sprigs and lemon wedges. Serve with whole wheat bread.

smoked salmon & wild arugula salad

ingredients

SERVES 4

1³/₄ oz/50 g wild arugula
   leaves
1 tbsp chopped fresh flat-leaf
   parsley
2 scallions, finely diced
2 large avocados
1 tbsp lemon juice
9 oz/250 g smoked salmon
lime wedges, to serve

lime mayonnaise

5 fl oz/150 ml/²/₃ cup
   mayonnaise
2 tbsp lime juice
finely grated rind of 1 lime
1 tbsp chopped fresh flat-leaf
   parsley, plus extra sprigs
   to garnish

method

1 Shred the arugula and arrange in 4 individual salad bowls or on 4 small plates. Sprinkle over the chopped parsley and scallions.

2 Halve, peel, and pit the avocados and cut into thin slices or small chunks. Brush with the lemon juice to prevent discoloration, then divide among the salad bowls. Mix together gently. Cut the smoked salmon into strips and sprinkle over the top.

3 Put the mayonnaise in a bowl, then add the lime juice and rind and the chopped parsley. Mix together well. Spoon some of the lime mayonnaise on top of each salad, garnish with parsley sprigs, and serve with lime wedges for squeezing over.

smoked fish salad

ingredients

SERVES 4

12 oz/350 g smoked haddock
    fillet, skinned

4 tbsp olive oil

1 tbsp lemon juice

2 tbsp sour cream

1 tbsp hot water

2 tbsp snipped fresh chives,
    plus extra to garnish

salt and pepper

1 plum tomato, peeled,
    seeded, and diced

8 quails' eggs

4 thick slices whole grain or
    multigrain bread

4 oz/115 g mixed salad greens

method

1 Fill a large skillet with water and bring to a boil. Add the smoked haddock fillet, cover, and remove the skillet from the heat. Let stand for 10 minutes until the fish is tender. Remove with a slotted spoon and drain on a plate. Flake the fish, removing and discarding any small bones. Set aside. Discard the cooking liquid.

2 Meanwhile, whisk the oil, lemon juice, sour cream, hot water, chives, salt, and pepper together in a pitcher. Stir in the tomato. Set aside.

3 Bring a small pan of water to a boil. Carefully lower the quails' eggs into the water and cook for 3–4 minutes from when the water returns to a boil (3 minutes for a slightly soft center, 4 minutes for a firm center). Drain at once and refresh under cold running water. Carefully shell the eggs, cut in half lengthwise and set aside.

4 Toast the bread and put a slice on each of 4 serving plates. Top with the salad greens, then the flaked fish and finally the quails' eggs. Spoon over the dressing and garnish with a few extra chives.

pasta niçoise

ingredients

SERVES 4

4 oz/115 g green beans, cut
    into 2-inch/5-cm lengths
8 oz/225 g dried fusilli tricolore
3$^1/_2$ fl oz/100 ml/generous
    $^1/_3$ cup olive oil
2 tuna steaks, about
    12 oz/350 g each
salt and pepper
6 cherry tomatoes, halved
2 oz/55 g/$^1/_3$ cup black olives,
    pitted and halved
6 canned anchovies, drained
    and chopped
3 tbsp chopped fresh
    flat-leaf parsley
2 tbsp lemon juice
8–10 radicchio leaves

method

1 Bring a large, heavy-bottom pan of lightly salted water to a boil. Add the green beans, reduce the heat, and cook for 5–6 minutes. Remove with a slotted spoon and refresh in a bowl of cold water. Drain well. Add the pasta to the same pan, return to a boil, and cook for 8–10 minutes, or until tender but still firm to the bite.

2 Meanwhile, brush a grill pan with some of the olive oil and heat until smoking. Season the tuna with salt and pepper and brush both sides with some of the remaining olive oil. Cook over medium heat for 2 minutes on each side, or until cooked to your liking, then remove from the grill pan and reserve.

3 Drain the pasta well and tip it into a bowl. Add the green beans, cherry tomatoes, olives, anchovies, parsley, lemon juice, and remaining olive oil and season with salt and pepper. Toss well and let cool. Remove and discard any skin from the tuna and slice thickly.

4 Gently mix the tuna into the pasta salad. Line a large salad bowl with the radicchio leaves, spoon in the salad, and serve.

tuna & two-bean salad

ingredients

SERVES 4–6

7 oz/200 g green beans

14 oz/400 g canned small
    white beans, such as
    cannellini, rinsed and
    drained

4 scallions, finely chopped

2 fresh tuna steaks, about
    8 oz/225 g each and
    ¾ inch/2 cm thick

olive oil, for brushing

9 oz/250 g cherry tomatoes,
    halved

lettuce leaves

fresh mint and parsley sprigs,
    to garnish

country-style crusty bread,
    to serve

dressing

handful of fresh mint leaves,
    shredded

handful of fresh parsley
    leaves, chopped

1 garlic clove, crushed

4 tbsp extra-virgin olive oil

1 tbsp red wine vinegar

salt and pepper

method

1 First, make the dressing. Put the mint leaves, parsley leaves, garlic, olive oil, and vinegar into a screw-top jar, add salt and pepper, and shake until blended. Pour into a large bowl and set aside.

2 Bring a pan of lightly salted water to a boil. Add the green beans and cook for 3 minutes. Add the white beans and cook for another 4 minutes until the green beans are tender-crisp and the white beans are heated through. Drain well and add to the bowl with the dressing and scallions. Toss together.

3 To cook the tuna, heat a stovetop ridged grill pan over high heat. Lightly brush the tuna steaks with oil, then season with salt and pepper. Cook the steaks for 2 minutes, then turn over and cook on the other side for an additional 2 minutes for rare or up to 4 minutes for well done.

4 Remove the tuna from the grill pan and let rest for 2 minutes, or until completely cool. When ready to serve, add the tomatoes to the bean mixture and toss lightly. Line a serving platter with lettuce leaves and pile on the bean salad. Flake the tuna over the top. Serve warm or at room temperature with plenty of bread, garnished with the herbs.

tuna & avocado salad

ingredients

SERVES 4

2 avocados, pitted, peeled,
and cubed

9 oz/250 g cherry tomatoes,
halved

2 red bell peppers, seeded
and chopped

1 bunch fresh flat-leaf
parsley, chopped

2 garlic cloves, crushed

1 fresh red chile, seeded and
finely chopped

juice of $1/2$ lemon

6 tbsp olive oil

pepper

3 tbsp sesame seeds

4 fresh tuna steaks, about
$5^{1}/_{2}$ oz/150 g each

8 cooked new potatoes, cubed

arugula leaves, to serve

method

1 Toss the avocados, tomatoes, red bell peppers, parsley, garlic, chile, lemon juice, and 2 tablespoons of the oil together in a large bowl. Season with pepper, cover, and let chill in the refrigerator for 30 minutes.

2 Lightly crush the sesame seeds in a mortar with a pestle. Tip the crushed seeds onto a plate and spread out. Press each tuna steak in turn into the crushed seeds to coat on both sides.

3 Heat 2 tablespoons of the remaining oil in a skillet, add the potatoes, and cook, stirring frequently, for 5–8 minutes, or until crisp and brown. Remove from the skillet and drain on paper towels.

4 Wipe out the skillet, add the remaining oil, and heat over high heat until very hot. Add the tuna steaks and cook for 3–4 minutes on each side.

5 To serve, divide the avocado salad among 4 serving plates. Top each with a tuna steak, then sprinkle over the potatoes and a handful of arugula leaves.

seafood & spinach salad

ingredients

SERVES 4

1 lb 2 oz/500 g live mussels,
  prepared (see page 38)
3¹/₂ oz/100 g raw shrimp,
  shelled and deveined
12 oz/350 g live scallops,
  shucked and cleaned
1 lb 2 oz/500 g baby spinach
  leaves
4 tbsp water
3 scallions, sliced
lemon wedges, to garnish

dressing

4 tbsp extra-virgin olive oil
2 tbsp white wine vinegar
1 tbsp lemon juice
1 tsp finely grated lemon rind
1 garlic clove, chopped
1 tbsp grated fresh gingerroot
1 small fresh red chile,
  seeded and sliced
1 tbsp chopped fresh cilantro,
  plus extra sprigs to garnish
salt and pepper

method

1 Put the mussels in a large pan with a little water and cook, covered, over high heat, shaking the pan occasionally, for 3–4 minutes, or until the mussels have opened. Discard any mussels that remain closed. Strain the mussels, reserving the cooking liquid.

2 Return the reserved cooking liquid to the pan and bring to a boil, add the shrimp and scallops, and cook for 3 minutes. Remove from the heat and drain. Remove the mussels from their shells. Refresh the mussels, shrimp, and scallops under cold running water, drain, and put them in a large bowl. Let cool, then cover with plastic wrap and let chill in the refrigerator for 45 minutes.

3 Meanwhile, rinse the spinach leaves and put them in a pan with the water. Cook over high heat for 1 minute. Transfer to a colander, refresh under cold running water, and drain.

4 To make the dressing, combine all the dressing ingredients in a small bowl. Divide the spinach among 4 serving dishes, then sprinkle over half the scallions. Top with the mussels, shrimp, and scallops, then sprinkle over the remaining scallions. Drizzle over the dressing, garnish with cilantro sprigs and lemon wedges, and serve.

coconut shrimp with cucumber salad

ingredients

SERVES 4

7 oz/200 g/1 cup brown basmati rice

$^{1}/_{2}$ tsp coriander seeds

2 egg whites, lightly beaten

3$^{1}/_{2}$ oz/100 g/generous $^{3}/_{4}$ cup dry unsweetened coconut

24 raw jumbo shrimp, shelled and tails left intact

$^{1}/_{2}$ cucumber

4 scallions, thinly sliced lengthwise

1 tsp sesame oil

1 tbsp finely chopped fresh cilantro

1 lime, cut into wedges, to garnish

method

1 Bring a large pan of water to a boil, add the rice, and cook for 25 minutes, or until tender. Drain and set aside in a strainer covered with a clean dish towel to absorb the steam.

2 Meanwhile, soak 8 wooden skewers in cold water for 30 minutes, then drain.

3 Crush the coriander seeds in a mortar with a pestle. Heat a nonstick skillet over medium heat and cook the seeds, turning, until they start to color. Tip onto a plate and set aside.

4 Put the egg whites into a shallow bowl and the coconut into a separate bowl. Roll each shrimp first in the egg whites, then in the coconut. Thread onto a skewer. Repeat so that each skewer is threaded with 3 coated shrimp.

5 Using a potato peeler, peel long strips from the cucumber to create ribbons, put into a strainer to drain, then toss with the scallions and oil in a bowl, and set aside.

6 Cook the shrimp under a broiler preheated to high for 3–4 minutes on each side, or until pink and slightly browned. Mix the rice with the coriander seeds and cilantro, press into 4 dariole molds and invert each mold onto a serving plate. Serve with cucumber salad and shrimp skewers, garnished with lime wedges.

shrimp & rice salad

ingredients

SERVES 4

6 oz/175 g/generous ¾ cup
    mixed long-grain
    and wild rice

12 oz/350 g cooked shelled
    shrimp

1 mango, peeled, pitted,
    and diced

4 scallions, sliced

1 oz/25 g/¼ cup slivered
    almonds

1 tbsp finely chopped fresh
    mint

pepper

dressing

1 tbsp extra-virgin olive oil

2 tsp lime juice

1 garlic clove, crushed

1 tsp honey

salt and pepper

method

1 Bring a large pan of lightly salted water to a boil. Add the rice, return to a boil, and cook for 35 minutes, or until tender. Drain, then transfer to a large bowl and stir in the shrimp.

2 To make the dressing, combine the olive oil, lime juice, garlic, and honey in a large pitcher, season with salt and pepper, and whisk until well blended. Pour the dressing over the rice and shrimp mixture and let cool.

3 Add the mango, scallions, almonds, and mint to the salad and season with pepper. Stir thoroughly, transfer to a large serving dish, and serve.

shrimp & papaya salad

ingredients

SERVES 4

1 papaya, peeled

12 oz/350 g large cooked
    shelled shrimp

assorted baby salad greens,
    to serve

dressing

4 scallions, chopped finely

2 fresh red chiles, seeded
    and chopped finely

1 tsp fish sauce

1 tbsp vegetable or peanut oil

juice of 1 lime

1 tsp jaggery or soft light
    brown sugar

method

1 Scoop the seeds out of the papaya and slice thinly. Stir gently together with the shrimp.

2 Mix the scallions, chiles, fish sauce, oil, lime juice, and sugar together.

3 Arrange the salad greens in a bowl and top with the papaya and shrimp. Pour the dressing over and serve immediately.

monkfish stir-fry

ingredients

SERVES 4

2 tsp sesame oil

1 lb/450 g monkfish steaks, cut
    into 1-inch/2.5-cm chunks

1 red onion, sliced thinly

3 cloves garlic, chopped finely

1 tsp grated fresh gingerroot

8 oz/225 g fine tip asparagus

6 oz/175 g/3 cups
    mushrooms, sliced thinly

2 tbsp soy sauce

1 tbsp lemon juice

lemon wedges, to garnish

cooked noodles, to serve

method

1 Heat the oil in a skillet over a medium-high heat. Add the fish, red onion, garlic, gingerroot, asparagus, and mushrooms. Stir-fry for 2–3 minutes.

2 Stir in the soy sauce and lemon juice and cook for another minute. Remove from the heat and transfer to warmed serving dishes.

3 Garnish with lemon wedges and serve immediately on a bed of cooked noodles.

stir-fried rice noodles with marinated fish

ingredients

SERVES 4

1 lb/450 g monkfish or cod, cubed

8 oz/225 g salmon fillets, cubed

2 tbsp vegetable or peanut oil

2 fresh green chiles, seeded and chopped

grated rind and juice of 1 lime

1 tbsp fish sauce

4 oz/115 g wide rice noodles

2 tbsp vegetable or peanut oil

2 shallots, sliced

2 garlic cloves, chopped finely

1 fresh red chile, seeded and chopped

2 tbsp Thai soy sauce

2 tbsp chili sauce

sprigs of cilantro, to garnish

method

1 Place the fish in a shallow bowl. To make the marinade, mix the oil, green chiles, lime juice and rind, and fish sauce together and pour over the fish. Cover and let chill for 2 hours.

2 Put the noodles in a bowl and cover with boiling water. Leave for 8–10 minutes (check the package instructions) and drain well.

3 Heat the oil in a wok or large skillet and sauté the shallots, garlic, and red chile until lightly browned. Add the soy sauce and chili sauce. Add the fish and the marinade to the wok and stir-fry gently for 2–3 minutes until cooked through.

4 Add the drained noodles and stir gently. Garnish with cilantro and serve immediately.

shrimp, snow pea & cashew nut stir-fry

ingredients

SERVES 4

3 oz/85 g/generous $1/2$ cup
   dry roasted cashew nuts

3 tbsp peanut oil

4 scallions, finely sliced

2 celery stalks, sliced thinly

3 carrots, sliced finely

100 g/$3^1/2$ oz baby corn cobs,
   halved

6 oz/175 g/3 cups
   mushrooms, sliced finely

1 clove of garlic,
   chopped coarsely

1 lb/450 g raw shrimp,
   shelled

1 tsp cornstarch

2 tbsp soy sauce

2 fl oz/50 ml/$1/4$ cup
   chicken stock

8 oz/225 g/2 cups savoy
   cabbage, shredded

6 oz/175 g/$1^3/4$ cups
   snow peas

cooked rice, to serve

method

1 Put a skillet over a medium heat and add the cashew nuts; toast them until they begin to brown. Remove with a slotted spoon and reserve.

2 Add the oil to the pan and heat. Add the scallions, celery, carrots, and baby corn cobs and cook, stirring occasionally, over medium-high heat for 3–4 minutes.

3 Add the mushrooms and cook until they become brown. Mix in the garlic and shrimp, stirring until the shrimp turn pink.

4 Mix the cornstarch smoothly with the soy sauce and chicken stock. Add the liquid to the shrimp mixture and stir. Then add the savoy cabbage, snow peas, and all but a few of the cashew nuts and cook for 2 minutes.

5 Garnish with the reserved cashew nuts and serve on a bed of rice.

salmon & scallops with cilantro & lime

ingredients

SERVES 4

6 tbsp peanut oil

10 oz/280 g salmon steak, skinned and cut into 1-inch/2.5-cm chunks

8 oz/225 g scallops

3 carrots, sliced thinly

2 celery stalks, cut into 1-inch/2.5-cm pieces

2 orange bell peppers, sliced thinly

6 oz/175 g/3 cups oyster mushrooms, sliced thinly

1 clove garlic, crushed

6 tbsp chopped fresh cilantro

3 shallots, sliced thinly

2 limes, juiced

1 tsp lime zest

1 tsp dried red pepper flakes

3 tbsp dry sherry

3 tbsp soy sauce

cooked noodles, to serve

method

1 In a wok or large frying pan, heat the oil over medium heat. Add the salmon and scallops, and stir-fry for 3 minutes. Remove from the pan, then set aside and keep warm.

2 Add the carrots, celery, bell peppers, mushrooms, and garlic to the wok and stir-fry for 3 minutes. Add the cilantro and shallots, and stir.

3 Add the lime juice and zest, dried red pepper flakes, sherry, and soy sauce and stir. Return the salmon and scallops to the wok and stir-fry carefully for another minute.

4 Serve immediately on a bed of cooked noodles.

scallops in black bean sauce

ingredients

SERVES 4

2 tbsp vegetable or peanut oil

1 tsp finely chopped garlic

1 tsp finely chopped fresh
  gingerroot

1 tbsp fermented black beans,
  rinsed and lightly mashed

14 oz/400 g scallops

$1/2$ tsp light soy sauce

1 tsp Shaoxing rice wine

1 tsp sugar

3–4 red Thai chiles,
  finely chopped

1–2 tsp chicken stock

1 tbsp finely chopped
  scallions

method

1 In a preheated wok or deep pan, heat the oil. Add the garlic and stir, then add the gingerroot and stir-fry together for about 1 minute, or until fragrant.

2 Mix in the black beans, then toss in the scallops and stir-fry for 1 minute. Add the light soy sauce, Shaoxing, sugar, and chiles.

3 Lower the heat and simmer for 2 minutes, adding the stock if necessary. Finally add the scallions, then stir and serve.

squid & red onion stir-fry

ingredients

SERVES 4

1 lb/450 g squid rings
2 tbsp all-purpose flour
$^1/_2$ tsp salt
1 green bell pepper
2 tbsp peanut oil
1 red onion, sliced
5$^3/_4$-oz/160-g jar black
    bean sauce

method

1 Rinse the squid rings under cold running water and pat dry with paper towels.

2 Place the all-purpose flour and salt in a bowl and mix together. Add the squid rings and toss until they are finely coated.

3 Using a sharp knife, seed the bell pepper and slice into thin strips.

4 Heat the peanut oil in a large preheated wok. Add the bell pepper and red onion to the wok and stir-fry for 2 minutes, or until the vegetables are just beginning to soften. Add the squid rings to the wok and cook for an additional 5 minutes, or until the squid is cooked through.

5 Add the black bean sauce to the wok and heat through until the juices are bubbling. Transfer to warmed bowls and serve at once.

sweet chile squid

ingredients

SERVES 4

1 tbsp sesame seeds

2 tbsp sesame oil

10 oz/280 g squid, cut into strips

2 red bell peppers, sliced thinly

3 shallots, sliced thinly

3 oz/85 g/1$\frac{1}{2}$ cups mushrooms, sliced thinly

1 tbsp dry sherry

4 tbsp soy sauce

1 tsp sugar

1 tsp hot chile flakes, or to taste

1 clove of garlic, crushed

1 tsp sesame oil

cooked rice, to serve

method

1 Place the sesame seeds on a cookie sheet and toast under a hot broiler, then set aside. Heat 1 tablespoon of oil in a skillet over a medium heat. Add the squid and cook for 2 minutes. Remove from the skillet and set aside.

2 Add the other tablespoon of oil to the skillet and cook the bell peppers and shallots over a medium heat for 1 minute. Add the mushrooms and cook for another 2 minutes.

3 Return the squid to the skillet and add the sherry, soy sauce, sugar, chile flakes, and garlic, stirring thoroughly. Cook for an additional 2 minutes.

4 Sprinkle with the toasted sesame seeds, then drizzle over the sesame oil and mix. Serve on a bed of rice.